GIVE ME TEA, PLEASE

ALSO WRITTEN BY NATASHA V. BROODIE

Swaggart: The Art of Professional Schmoozing at Job Interviews
November 2023

GIVE ME
TEA
please

PRACTICAL INGREDIENTS
FOR TASTEFUL LANGUAGE

natasha & broodie

AMADIO™
New York

ISBN: 979-8-9893541-1-5 (Paperback)

To protect the privacy of certain individuals the names and identifying details have been changed.

Front cover image and book design by Natasha Velisha Broodie. Interior illustrations by Canva.

Printed in the United States of America.
Second printing edition 2024.
First printing edition 2021.

AMADIO™
6614 Avenue U
PMB 96283
Brooklyn, NY 11234
www.LifeWithTheBigE.com

Give Me Tea, Please
Practical Ingredients for Tasteful Language

How to use the English you already know
more professionally

To my Russian, French and Egyptian clients who taught me so much about their language and culture whilst I shared mine.

To every person of color securing their bread and butter in corporate hell…

And to Mom.

CONTENTS

PART TWO: HOW TO, FROM A TEA SOMMELIER. 37

AFTERWARD. 75

REFERENCES 87

PREFACE

On Petrovka Street in Moscow, Russia, there is a casual and cozy restaurant called LavkaLavka. This restaurant was one of the first victims of my limited foreign language skills. In severely broken Russian, I asked the waitress, "How do I order tea in Russian?"

"There are many ways that you can do this," she said with patient amusement. She quickly recited a few different constructions. None of them sounded familiar to the examples on the apps such as Learn Russian - 5000 Phrases by Fun Easy Learn or DuoLingo. But then she said, *"Dayte chay, pozhaluysta."*

Yes... I remembered this from DuoLingo, thank you very much! And yes... I could recall this from MasterRussian.com. *Well, surely that proves that the site is reliable!*

"Ok. *Dayte chay, pozhaluysta. Spasibo!*"

With a pleasing nod, she smiled and walked away. *Dayte chay, pozhaluysta*: give me tea, please. *Give me. Give me? Give me tea? Surely there must be a more polite way to ask for something,* I thought. *Give me... This sounds too demanding. What if they don't want to give me tea? What if someone is having a really bad day and interprets my innocent request as a pesky demand? What if I get that look that my mom always gave me when I spoke outside of the Caribbean Center of Morality and Ethics.* (Only a Caribbean child would know how dangerous this could be). So a few days later, I found the "polite version": *ya by khotela chay pozhaluysta.* Surely the longer construction would be received more favorably. After memorizing the phrase, I tried to use it immediately.

The next victim was Cafe Shelby, just a block north of Gorky Park. Its spacious layout explores a vibrant clash between a collection of sporty racing car relics set against a flirty purple canvas. The soft-spoken staff welcomed my limited Russian skills graciously. But after too many failed attempts to modify my accent, the "polite version" succumbed to the simple phrase, *"Dayte chay, pozhaluysta."* A dawn of comprehension was followed by a simple smile. And a few minutes later, I had my tea.

Even though months have now passed, saying in Russian, "Give me tea, please," still feels uncomfortable and demanding. However, in Russian etiquette, this is perfectly normal and acceptable. **No offense given, none taken.**

... And yet, this is not the case when speaking English.

To say, "Give me tea, please," **falls short** of etiquette standards used across the English-speaking world. We can say, *"Dayte chay, pozhaluysta,"* with suitable intonations and still be received respectfully amongst Russian speakers. **On the other hand**, we cannot say, "Give me tea, please," and still be received courteously in the English-speaking world. Regardless of speaking softly or using unusually high-pitched tones, "give me" is too direct to be considered proper etiquette.

So, therein lies a common problem for non-native English speakers across the globe: how do you translate words into English without neglecting tone or compromising meaning? To learn how to think, speak, and write more effectively in English, the following pages explore the usages of and differences between formal, informal, direct, and indirect language.

Give Me Tea, Please: Practical Ingredients for Tasteful Language, is a guidebook that is written especially for learners of English as a Foreign Language (EFL). The guidebook is particularly useful for business professionals who work in an international environment, at a global company, or with an international organization. Similarly, **whether or not** one is a non-native English speaker who must use English **from time to time,** all business professionals working in international environments may find this guidebook resourceful and practical.

I wrote *Give Me Tea, Please,* with a conscious effort to simplify the language of this guidebook. As such, this guidebook is suitable for intermediate-level EFL students and above. The guidebook is designed so that EFL learners can easily understand how to improve their written and spoken skills while acquiring new professional vocabulary for their careers.

This guidebook is not meant to teach English! Instead, I provide simple templates and proven strategies on how to use the English that you already know more effectively. Furthermore, at the end of the guidebook, there is an appendix called, *The Encyclopedia of Professional Communication*. This appendix is a simplified dictionary of each word formatted in bold-typeface and should become part of every EFL student's spoken vocabulary.

INTRODUCTION

In 2016, the World Economic Forum published a report by Kai L. Chan, Distinguished Fellow at the INSEAD Innovation and Policy Initiative. In the report titled, *These Are the Most Powerful Languages in the World*, English ranked as number one on the list.

There are debates as to which language is the most widely spoken foreign language in the world. While Mandarin **dominates** the globe with over 1.2 billion speakers, it is constantly challenged by English as the **go-to** language for international communication. Therefore, as our world today continues to **globalize** in politics, economics, societal norms, and world religions, discussions on these matters at the international level are regularly **conducted** in English.

In 2013, the British Council **estimated** that over 1.5 billion students are learning English as a second language. **Comparatively**, only 180 million people are learning Mandarin as a foreign language.

In their report, *The English Effect,* the British Council **projected** that two billion people will speak English by 2020. This will be approximately a quarter of the global population. So, Mandarin may be the most spoken language in the world (particularly by native speakers). However, the rising number of English language learners reflects the growing demand for international markets to use the Queen's English for global communication. It may indeed be time to learn English. And who knows, perhaps during the next century, international relations may favor a new language as the leader of global communication.

I wrote *Give Me Tea, Please,* with the aim to contribute to bridging communication gaps across cultures in diverse English-speaking environments. As more international businesses **lean on** English for global affairs, non-native English-speaking colleagues and clients are **liable** to overlook how their English communication continues to be misunderstood, misinterpreted, or poorly received. So, now you have a guidebook!

In the first half of the guidebook, you will find theories and explanations of the cultural logic in English-speaking regions. These perspectives are very much influenced by Caribbean, American, and British cultures and customs, which are the three strongest influences in my background. Then, the second part of the guidebook is practical and instructive by using a methodological and hands-on approach. You will be able to see how each theory from *Part One* is **put into practice** in *Part Two.*

Lastly, many times in this guidebook, you will find that I directly address people of color and members of **protected classes**. Were it not for the new global wave of populism and bigotry, I would write and provide suggestions without filtering. Based on experience working with racist, sexist, and ageist colleagues in exceptionally toxic professional environments, I have taken precautionary measures to provide additional advice to marginalized groups whenever possible. I write directly to these groups with the hope that one day, in a more equal and inclusive era, these highlighted suggestions will prove irrelevant and outdated.

So let this guidebook help you craft your speech in English to protect yourself against such harmful colleagues and precarious conditions in the work environment.

My very best wishes to all.

PART ONE

THE RECIPE AND INGREDIENTS

KEEP IT SIMPLE. KEEP IT SAFE.

Many years ago, I wrote what was perhaps my first and last exceptionally humiliating email. The construction of the email had been so poorly worded that its vivid memory sent nightmarish chills down my back for months afterward. Even now, I still shake my head in utter shame. For days, I trembled with unemployment anxiety, believing that the rise to my ultimate career goal was now thwarted by my own foolish making. What made it worse was my intention had been honorable. Sort of...

One of the worst managers on the planet was working at my office. Clearly unpopular, this **challenging colleague** left a mood of **corrosive** despair lingering between all floors of the building. Similar to many offices across the globe, during the colleague's absence, a childlike return to giggles, jokes, and backhanded whispers **pervaded** the stairwells and toilet stalls like ministerial **brush-bys**. From the most senior-ranking members in the office to the lowest of the lot, dignity was not spared for this colleague's reputation. Ludicrous stories about the colleague's extra-collegial affairs still trigger squeamishly terrible and vividly awkward images in my **mind's eye**; every retelling by shameless colleagues was performed like a pundit on late-night TV. Unsurprisingly, as fate would have it, I became the colleague's new Special Assistant.

Whenever someone would ask me what my new fancy job was, I would say that I babysat a pet dragon. Thinking that I had an unusually monstrous toddler to care for, inquirers would always follow up by asking, "Oh wow, how old is the child?" "Oh, I dunno," I would say. "I'd guess about 60...going on 60-something." But the tears of laughter never quite seemed to **reframe** the reality of going into the pitfall of fire and brimstone day after day to confront my dragon.

When it was time for the dragon to fly back to the keep, I tried to arrange a goodbye gathering. Completely forgetting that our team's grouped email addresses also contained the pet dragon's inbox, I wrote: "Even though we all didn't like this colleague, it would still be nice to properly say farewell…"

Or something like that.

A lesson learned from the horrid experience was to be careful of what you put in emails—and quadruple check to whom they're sent! As I always say to my clients, "It's better **to err on the side of caution**." Don't send an email unless its tone is neutral, instructive, or positive. Always.

THE FOUR TONAL CATEGORIES IN PROFESSIONAL COMMUNICATION

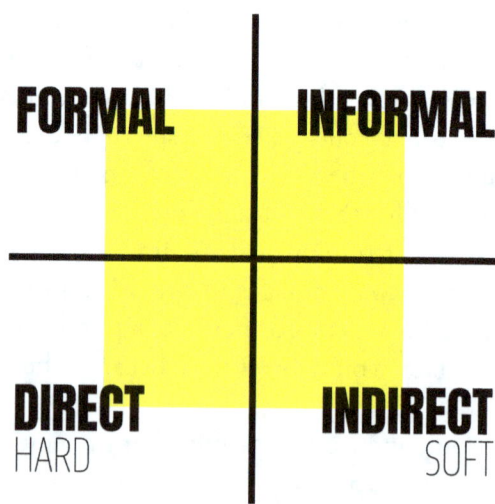

FORMAL   INFORMAL

DIRECT   INDIRECT
HARD   SOFT

My mistake above boils down to an unhealthy mixture of stupidity and naivety. Yet, avoiding collegial **blunders** in professional communication can be tricky even when **you have your head on your shoulders**. Additionally, as non-native English speakers, you have many more opportunities for verbal and written *faux pas!* Even for native English speakers, I find that common **missteps** occur when one must determine the relationship level with his or her colleagues. Whether a colleague is your **peer** or a career step above or below your position, selecting the proper tonal response is key to maintaining healthy and functioning professional relationships. Surely this concept is known. The question is: how do you ensure you get there?

Well, before you get there, ask yourself about your professional relationship dynamics. Are you friends with your colleagues, or are they simply unknown co-workers? Do you work with professional adversaries or report to a demon in the flesh? Has your career position changed into a collegial competitor? Do you work with bullies, tenured harassers, and law-evasive discriminators? Are ageism and condescension reflected in biases between junior and senior staff? Are you bound to a toxic environment, or do you tread through the waters of uncertainty day-to-day? Are your colleagues more than acquaintances with one another, or is the environment a lingering gloom of volcanic disruption?

Collegial interactions may vary based on social indicators. For example, top-down interactions may differ from the bottom-up. As non-native English speakers, I advise you to be wary of times when additional social indicators, which are listed under protected classes, change the nature of communication between colleagues. Based on your position on the **corporate ladder** and taking into consideration your status under a protected class, I would urge all to keep your language simple and safe until you master—truly master—the art of professional communication, which includes intonations! In both spoken and written English, poorly chosen diction can quickly raise tensions between communicators.

Find your voice. Know who you are and how you want to be received. Then allow your style of communication to be reflected in the tonal categories.

Therefore, understanding the principles of professional communication begins with recognizing four tonal categories. These tonal categories are formal, informal, direct, and indirect language. Whether you are a senior manager or the office cleaner, your goal as a professional communicator is to remain formal and indirect at all times. I repeat: your goal as a professional communicator is to remain FORMAL and INDIRECT. What a challenge!

You must master the ability to move **fluidly** between these four tonal categories. Your diction must become as selective and strategic as possible to obtain the result that you want. The question "Will you give me the report by 4 p.m.?" has a very different emotional impact than "Let's review the final version at 4 p.m." In contrast to cultures where direct language is masked by intonations and word endings, there is nothing like this in the English language. The English-speaking world simply does not share this flexibility. Perhaps that is why this concept is one of the trickiest to understand, accept, and master. You must choose your words wisely.

As you continue to build your vocabulary and diversify your syntax, your sentences will gradually become longer and more complex. Until you have mastered the basics, I suggest all non-advanced English-learning students stick to simple and compound sentence formation; seven to thirteen words per sentence **should do the trick**.

LANGUAGE REVIEW

A SIMPLE SENTENCE is a complete sentence containing one subject, one verb, and one object (predicate). Keep it simple! Grammatically speaking, a simple sentence is ONE independent clause. The latter definition is better because it allows you to quickly spot the main verb and its subject in a sentence before all the other grammatical forms are used. For example, the other grammatical forms may be prepositional phrases and relative clauses.

A COMPOUND SENTENCE is when two sentences are connected by a conjunction. Common conjunctions are "and," "but," "or," "nor," "for," "so," and "yet."

A COMPLEX SENTENCE is constructed by using subordinate clauses. Using subordinate clauses transforms ordinary sentences into eloquent prose. They often begin with Linking Words such as "despite," "in spite of," "although," "as," "because," etc. Stick with single and compound sentences for now if you are not yet an advanced speaker. Remember, seven to thirteen words per sentence should do the trick!

Mind your Ps and Qs.

FORMAL LANGUAGE

A young British woman on YouTube made a video about how to construct formal and polite language in the English-speaking world. In the examples that she gave, each request had well over 10 words per sentence in order to convey politeness. It's true; English is unlike other languages where formality is implied by particular pronouns and word endings. Instead, in English, it is common to use many words just to express kindness, sympathy, politeness, and respect.

Remember the story from the beginning of the guidebook? What if I had asked in English, "Can I have tea?" This question is not disrespectful when asked with suitable intonations. Contextually, reading this question would not necessarily **raise any eyebrows** either. However, it is difficult to argue that the following examples are anything but respectful and polite in written or oral form:

"May I please have a cup of tea?"

"I would be grateful for a cup of tea, please."

The examples have 8 and 10 words each, **respectively**. The difference in tone between the first question and the latter examples is based on modals. A key difference between a formal tone and an informal tone is the use of modals. Mastering the use of modals will instantly soften your language and move your written tone into formal speech. Beware though, extreme use of formal language is liable to come off as bone-dry, stiff, and hollow. To **counterbalance** this, varying your intonations can help. As a stickler for using formal language in all business communication, I often find it necessary to vary my intonations in oral speech in order to eliminate **perfunctory** mannerisms. By doing so, formal language feels more approachable and inviting.

In the next chapter, we'll examine and construct workable templates for you to use later on for additional practice. For now, let's take a look at some quick examples below. How would you ask a colleague for the report on the company's quarterly **earnings**? Or, how would you ask a colleague for any item that you want in the office for your assignments? Often, when I **propose** similar questions to my clients, they form responses similar to these:

"Can you give me the report on our quarterly earnings?"

"Do you want to meet next week?"

"What happened during the meeting with X client and Y client?"

Although there are Business English books that support this construction as polite language, I strongly suggest to non-native English speakers to err on the side of caution! Consider rephrasing these requests with the polite form of modals instead of the familiar form of modals. Using a polite modal will change the tone and feel of your request instantly. The request instantly softens. In the English-speaking world, polite modal words and phrases convey humility and respect. You can never be too polite in a professional environment! Remember that English is globalizing; different cultures, genders, and ages are using English to engage inside the same office environment. With your own culture **at the helm of** how you process social interactions, understand that there are many more opportunities to be misunderstood in English—even with the best intentions. So, unless you are very familiar with your colleagues and regularly lunch with them informally, err on the side of caution and use polite modals!

Another reason why modals are crucial to professional communication is because of their strategic function; simply put, modals propose suggestions and possibilities, which gently **sow the seeds** of your desires into your receiver's head. This concept will prove to be key when you are in the section called, Request A Meeting in *Part Two* of this guidebook. As the receiver of the request, one does not have to accept the proposal. Instead, the receiver **retains** the option to reject the proposal. The question or statement that has been formed by a polite modal is just a suggestion...just another option...just another possibility to consider. From my experience, when making meeting requests using polite modals, the receiver more often than not accepts the proposal (my planted seed), or makes slight adjustments to my request in order to accept with minimal back and forth correspondence.

Therefore, the receiver (who may or may not be aware of this strategy's effect), has the impression that he or she is in control of the outcome of the request, when in reality, you have planted the seed in your receiver's minds in a gentle and indirect way. He or she has been asked to provide their preference regarding your request. The receiver could say, "yes" to the proposal and respond favorably to your proposition. The receiver also has the option to say, "no" and to reject the proposal entirely. As colleagues hustle alongside peers, managers, and mentors, it's a rare and appreciated gesture to have our thoughts and perspectives considered. So proposing your requests with polite modals positions you as an approachable and team-oriented colleague while ensuring your true needs are met and considered. **Try it out** in *Part Two*. See how it goes.

After teaching this concept to one of my Russian clients at L'Oréal, she was pleased to recognize **a stark difference** in communication with one of her regular external clients. During our next lesson, I think she expressed that the reply email seemed "happy". I started laughing.

Now yes, you might be thinking: I don't have time to risk receiving a rejection to my request; I need a decision to be made now! I hear you. Here is the last justification for why a "modal-backed" approach is helpful for your career advancement. In cultures like the U.S. and U.K., **taking the initiative** is a professional character trait that is usually appreciated (though not always). By proposing what you want with polite modals, you have taken the initiative by saving the receiver from engaging in time-consuming **back-and-forth** emailing just to arrive at a similar conclusion. So instead, make a kind proposal. Extend the **courtesy** to your receiver; give him or her the option to agree or make a new proposition.

During the many years that I worked as an Executive Assistant, I learned **midway through the game** that when I requested appointments on behalf of XYZ and used polite modals to temper the request, the response was rarely ever anything but agreeable. Oh, what a time-saver! Polite modals give the receiver the option to say yes or no, while you remain in control by requesting exactly what you want or need in return. Should you need to propose a request, then state exactly what you are after by proposing the request with a polite form of modals. We'll see some examples in the section called, *Three Types of Communication.*

In summary, when working with reasonable clients and colleagues, if you propose a solution in your query email, the recipient is more likely to follow along and agree to your terms or request. From my experience, the only times that I have received an alternative proposition is when the recipient has foreseen an **operational challenge**.

I say again that I strongly believe that modals are important to master because multiple cultures are now using English for global communication. This means that there are multiple opportunities to misuse terms and words when regional dialects are translated into English. Every culture has its own form of conveying respect, which often cannot so easily be translated into English words. The last thing that you want to do is lose a business opportunity or have negotiations fail because your external colleague(s), client(s), or customer(s) believed you were too pushy or disrespectful. Remember, because the world is globalizing, more companies, organizations, and entrepreneurs are using English as the go-to language for business communication. You must modify your written and oral tonal vocabulary. Master the use of modals.

LANGUAGE REVIEW

MODAL VERBS are particular verbs that are used to express probability, permission and advice. These verbs are key to speaking with formality, politeness and respect. A table of both familiar and polite modal verbs is below.

FORMAL	POLITE
CAN	COULD
WILL	WOULD
SHALL	SHOULD

MUST   MIGHT   MAY

Be careful of what you say to people.
A friend today can be an enemy tomorrow.

INFORMAL LANGUAGE

Often, I've wondered about how to have a genuine personality in an office environment when so many of these spaces are breeding grounds for ruthless competitors. More often than not, when money, reputation, and collegial **clout** are at stake, the office environment morphs into an unrelenting Reality TV sit-com of viral **gossip** and manipulative support. **Steering clear** from corporate **honey traps** designed to **stagnate** or **demote** your professional advancement may mean a daily dose of isolation and awkwardness, particularly for those who are people of color and for those represented by a protected class. Add a healthy mixture of bigotry, and **the tangled web** of sabotage thickens.

For readers who are people of color or identify under a protected class, I cannot express enough the importance of **toeing the line**. Do not give reason to support claims that favor a bigot's insecurities about you. You and your professional opposition are not allies. You will never be allies. When someone shows you precisely who they are, e.g., their moral code, their values, or their behaviors, make no excuses for it. Believe what you have seen and let no one dismiss your experience. Genuine actions never deceive.

In a nutshell, be careful of using informal language with colleagues, particularly if you are a member of a protected class. These are the best opportunities to take even your kindest of gestures and **twist them up** in order to suit a bigot's end game.

My advice is not meant to suggest that it is impossible to make sincere and lasting relationships with colleagues at work. Even still, let us never forget that the old adage remains true today: the love of money is the root of all evil. In the context of building strong relationships at work, when money is the principal driving force behind one's professional decision-making, a colleague may not hesitate **to throw you under the bus** in order to protect a job or advance in the field. Err on the side of caution!

So in order to toe the line very carefully, I sadly advise people of color and members of protected classes to always remain formal and professional.

If you are lucky enough to work in a safe and collegial environment, then you may be at liberty to practice informal language at work. Because idioms, **colloquialisms**, and other forms of popular expressions vary in tone and are difficult to interpret from **face value**, I advise again to triple check with native English speakers on the impression and reception of these literary devices. If you wish to use expressions in order to grow your social vocabulary at work or to sound more like a native English speaker, then I urge all to find a friendly peer at work who is either fluent in English or speaks English with near-native English fluency (C1/C2 level) and review how the expression is received in real life.

THE ABSENCE OF MODALS

As formal language is defined by using polite modals, informal language is defined as the absence of modals. We know informal language is spoken with our peers, friends, and in some cultures within families. We can detect informal language when listening to intonations. But what does informal language look like on paper? What defines writing as informal, especially when the communicator is represented by words rather than by sounds?

Phrasal verbs, popular expressions, colloquialisms, and idioms are all common forms of informal language. You have already seen some of these grammatical forms used in this book and highlighted in bold-typeface. As these forms of informal language are generally learned by living in English-speaking cultures, an alternative method to learn them is to become a strategic reader.

A strategic reader means not only to digest relevant material for his or her industry but also to adapt reading materials in order to improve one's written and oral communication. Therefore, strategic reading is the process of targeting specific vocabulary (like **buzz words**), grammatical constructions (like phrasal verbs), syntax, and diction that would be the most useful, influential, and common for one's industry and professional level. For example, if your aim is to improve recognizing and using phrasal verbs, I do not suggest finding a list of these grammatical constructions and memorizing them. This is because a single phrasal verb can have multiple meanings that have no association with one another. There are hundreds if not thousands of phrasal verbs! A closer look below demonstrates how one phrasal verb can be informal and indirect while the same phrasal verb, which may be used in a different context, can be direct in tone or used as slang. So let's look at the phrasal verb: **TAKE OUT**.

Take out (a verb):
to request a temporary loan such as books, money, etc.

Take out (an imperative):
to ask someone to remove items from a location.

Take out (a verb):
to accompany someone or something.

Take out (a verb and popular expression):
to ask someone to go on a date with you.

Take out (used as a noun):
the food that you purchase in a restaurant in order to take it home.

Can you imagine memorizing five distinctly different meanings for one phrasal verb alongside a list of 1,000 phrasal verbs? That task might be daunting for some. For me, when I learn foreign languages,

I refrain from studying vocabulary rotas as they are absolutely useless and demotivating—just pure poison to my language-loving soul; my learning style is extremely physical. Similarly, for those who are also kinesthetic learners, there might be an easier and more practical way to learn and expand terminology. Find reading material that reflects the dialogues you are most likely to have at work or that reflects your general interests. For me, for example, this would be dialogues and articles on global humanitarian crises, the arts, culture, or travel. Then, target all the phrasal verbs in the article. After locating them, use each phrasal verb **as soon as possible** by retaining the same meaning and the same grammatical construction in your next report, email, or spoken conversation. This should help you build a stronger active vocabulary in phrasal verbs.

As I continue to learn languages in the regions of my target languages, I have noticed that phrasal verbs are chiefly an English language device. Whereas parts of speech are often shared between foreign languages, phrasal verbs are a grammatical construction that is uniquely English. Out of all the languages that I've studied, I have never seen any foreign language whose syntax comprises something even remotely close to phrasal verbs. Therefore, mastery of this **peculiar** grammatical device becomes more difficult without **a game plan**. I advocate practicing strategic reading; Pick a topic of interest and scout for phrasal verbs. With this approach, you can also acquire new idioms and popular expressions too.

Next, let's look at idioms in the workplace. For starters, idioms may be popular expressions, but not all popular expressions are idioms. Most idioms are informal, but not all idioms are indirect. Some idioms can be commanding and accusatory in meaning or tone. These idioms are very direct—too direct for professional communication! Remember, your goal as a professional communicator is to remain formal and indirect as much as possible. So therein lies a problem for when you want to expand your use of idiomatic language; which idioms are appropriate for professional communication and which are not?

Selecting the best idioms to use on the job requires recognizing the idiom as either formal, informal, direct, or indirect in tone

For professionals in junior-level positions, I suggest building an idiomatic database of only formal and indirect idioms. For professionals in executive-level positions, I advise you to build both formal and informal idiomatic expressions, and I suggest you refrain from using any idiom that is direct. A **general rule of thumb** is that idiomatic expressions suitable for the workplace all have one thing in common: they are all positive, uplifting, motivating, and agreeable in nature.

In saying that, I encourage non-native English speakers—particularly those who are people of color—to err on the side of caution and first check with a native English speaker on how the idiom **in question** will be culturally received by colleagues in the work environment. Again, be very careful to avoid aiding bigots **in sheep's clothing**, who desire to characterize your collegial interactions as aggressive, defensive, or victimizing.

Similarly, popular expressions can be tricky to **nail down**, especially for professional use. Like idioms, popular expressions can help your communication sound more relaxed and cultured. Unlike idioms, popular expressions are often less figurative in meaning and are more informal. Before using a popular expression, check with a native English speaker on its meaning.

Remember, a phrasal verb can have multiple meanings, whereas idioms and popular expressions have one. Because it may be difficult to locate new idioms and popular expressions in spoken and written form, purchase a book or use online resources that list the meaning for each expression. Then, use strategic reading to help naturalize the expressions in your day-to-day vocabulary.

Lastly, whether you are writing formal or informal content, you may mix informal language devices with modals and still be received well. This tactic allows language to feel not only respectful and polite but also welcoming and approachable. If you must write purely formal prose, which occurs most often in contracts or in other legal documents, then eliminate informal devices altogether and adhere strictly to formal language.

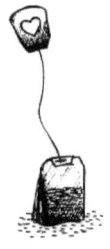

LANGUAGE REVIEW

A PHRASAL VERB is a verb paired with a preposition. Anytime you see a verb directly followed by a preposition, note that you have most likely just read a phrasal verb. A phrasal verb can also appear as a short phrase that begins with a verb and ends with a preposition.

An IDIOM is a figurative expression whose meaning is different from the literal meaning of each word.

An EXPRESSION is a common phrase populated by a society, a community, or a culture.

Make no bones about it!

DIRECT LANGUAGE

YOU. WHAT. WANT.

No other word, in *The Encyclopedia of Professional Communication*, is more powerful than the word **YOU**. Coming in at second place is the word **WHAT**. And lastly, **WANT** is similarly disastrous. These three words, when used in professional communication, have the rare and distinct power to cripple, destroy, and sack those who use them unwisely or carelessly. Use them with extreme caution. Avoid them **at all costs**.

When YOU, WHAT, and WANT are used with the main verb, the communication becomes too direct for most English-speaking communities. Therefore, in professional environments, one must rephrase the request so that the language becomes more indirect. (In the next section called *On Indirect Language*, we'll see how to do this). "Why," you might ask. Unlike other languages such as French, Spanish, and Russian, there are no conjugated forms reserved in English grammar to imply formality or politeness. *Vous* has no counterpart in English. There is no direct translation for *Ustedes* or *Vosotros*. Similarly, neither can *Вы* be translated. There are no suffixes and word endings in English that are conjugated in order to reflect the Second-Person Plural form. As such, languages that honor formality by using a separate grammatical form fall short when they are translated into English because this grammatical concept simply does not exist in English logic.

YOU will always be received as a point of attack or direct criticism. A colleague's back will stiffen, a junior staff member will **be crossed**, a senior manager will be affronted if the word YOU is used with just the right amount of perceived negativity—even if the statement was neutral or positive. Perhaps due to the common expression, "**fake it till you make it**," the growing lack of sincerity in collegial environments often causes colleagues to question their peers' integrity.

So, how does one know if the use of YOU is too direct? If the main verb can be absorbed by the pronoun YOU, then the sentence or statement is too direct. In other words, if the main verb becomes **peremptory**, then the tone is in danger of sounding accusatory and impolite.

"You left the report on my desk."

WHAT is often felt as abrasive as it sounds, especially when it's used alone. WHAT can mean, "I don't understand." WHAT can mean, "Why?" WHAT can ask about your needs. WHAT can also imply that something is wrong. Simply put, WHAT has many variations—too many. They are all very direct, and their meanings imply some manner of questioning the examiner. Therefore, WHAT may be received very harshly, **like a blunt ax**. There are more formal and professional ways to ask or say WHAT.

WANT has a similar yet slightly different feeling. As the least damaging of the three, WANT gives the receiver the impression of neediness. When WANT is the main verb of the sentence, any pronoun used alongside it implies a certain air of dependency from the person who is making the request. Neediness. Dependency. I believe these are the last feelings in the world that a colleague wants to experience from another colleague. When self-sufficiency and independence are qualities sought after by hiring managers and respected by teammates, WANTs interfere with these desirable character traits. So, just like the above, there are more clever and indirect ways to get what you want in a professional environment without saying WANT.

Moreover, in addition to YOU, WHAT, and WANT, the most dangerous tonal combination occurs when one combines informal tone with direct language. This combination is nothing more than unprofessional communication. Do not drink from this lethal cup—ever! This combination expresses, **in no uncertain terms**, that the speaker is accountable to no one. This combination is designed chiefly to offend, infuriate, and dehumanize the listener, the reader, or the receiver. Sadly, there are colleagues who are able to get away with such behavior.

Now, does this mean that YOU, WHAT, and WANT will never be words used in an office space? Does it mean if you read an email that asks, "Do you want to meet on Wednesday at 16:15," then the sender was trying to insult you? Of course not! As you become more proficient at **reading an environment**, expanding colloquialisms, and improving your intonations, you will gain more insight as to when and how to use YOU with a main verb. Even now, as a native English speaker who is proficient in oral and written communication, I still try to eliminate YOU, WHAT, and WANT from professional communication.

So what does direct communication look like? Well, let's first look at what direct language isn't.

We know that **uninhibited** communication is widely admired and encouraged. The lack of **hesitation** whilst communicating expresses one's fluency in subject matter and language. **Be that as it may**, articulation becomes **marred** when the language is impregnated with derogatory expressions. This is not direct language; this is rude language. **Funnily enough**, during numerous interviews that I've sat through, headhunters would caution me that the person to whom I would report has a reputation for "being very direct."

"No, I wouldn't say he's a screamer, **per se**... We have placed people in this office before, and they've stayed."

"Ok," I would say. "And how many of those placements report directly to him?"

"Well, this is the first time that we have been **retained** to scout for this position. He is nice—we've never had a complaint about physical harassment or anything like that. And remember, we are your HR manager; you can always come to us."

"You seem like someone who is hard to bully. I'm sure that you'll be able to handle her."

"Handle her?" And now I'm curious because I know that I'm not taking this job. "How many have sat in this position up till now?"

"O, that's a good question… I'm not sure exactly how many… Let me check and come back to you on that."

I had developed a thoroughly solid reputation for handling bullying, harassment, and discrimination in the workforce whilst still remaining at jobs for **the long haul**. In addition to submitting strong performance reviews and feedback to headhunters from my former ranking colleagues and supervisors, I could sit interviews confidently because my art of interviewing was always extremely focused and detailed. Headhunters knew that I was a serious candidate with years of relevant experience to back it. One would think these traits would **work in my favor**. But, I soon realized that it was an ever-present vulnerability.

Putting two and two together after sitting through countless interviews, I realized that headhunters were retained by some of the worst, high-profile clients on the planet. These clients all seem to have had an endless list of complaints about their lack of professionalism and less than collegial behavior. Powerful though they may be, problematic employers have always been ruthless to colleagues, and so they often find it difficult to secure long-term hires.

Perhaps for this reason, scouting out the right candidate becomes crucial; it's financially **lucrative** for all parties when a candidate displays commitment to the role—**no matter what**. But the selected candidate is liable to enter into a toxic work environment… So then what should happen? Should one stay in the job? **Not my cup of tea**…and hopefully never will be again!

Upon reflection, I had spent more than half of my daily life with these creepy, professionally insecure, and power-hungry colleagues who made it seem like I had either never left junior high school or entered into Dante's lowest level of purgatory. When professional daily life carefully details an object lesson on the abuse of power, the alacrity to perform above and beyond the job description loses significance. Engaging with toxic colleagues in toxic environments is like trying to escape from quicksand; the more one struggles to free oneself, the faster one sinks into the pit. And the less that one fights against the current, the slower one soul succumbs to its death. These experiences made me truly understand what direct language is and what it is not: Colleagues who are powerfully influential and yet never reduce their character by using forms of intimidation in order to procure what they want always build a timeless and infallible reputation as a strong leader. Their legacy becomes legendary.

For the purpose of the guidebook, I define direct language as stating facts and concerns with positive or neutral non-emotional language. When direct language is delivered in any other way, the communicator puts himself or herself at risk.

If communication is impregnated with derogatory language or negative adjectives—especially if the language insults or criticizes the receiver or audience—then the tone becomes **overtly** offensive. However, one chooses to characterize emotionally charged and offensive communication in the work environment, we understand that it lacks all forms of professionalism. Swearing, cursing, insults, and pejoratives are all forms of sordid language.

Moreover, the most dangerous combination of tones is when informal language is mixed up in direct language. This combination is combustible: a sleeping dragon waiting to be provoked and baited. Informal and direct communication is generally received as 100 percent unprofessional, whether used between peers, from a top-down approach, or vice versa. As I've said repetitively, this is not direct language; this is rude language! When rude language is characterized as direct language, the power of truly effective and direct communication loses its **agency**.

ACTIVE VOICE

So, how does one form direct communication while avoiding direct words like YOU, WHAT, and WANT? As non-native English speakers, this may be difficult to learn, particularly for those who come from a culture that uses directness freely. If your goal is to become better at using direct communication in a professional environment, then I advocate the following:

Use Active Voice construction, yet avoid using the Second-Person Singular form. Let's see an example:

BE WARY OF:
Your report was terrible. I was expecting more details, but this draft was useless. It did not sound like you put any effort into it. What happened? You had three weeks to complete it. Now we need to push back the entire deadline for the team because I need to find someone else to do this instead of you.

TRY THIS:
Perhaps we can discuss the latest version of this report. I believe that the draft can be more substantiated if there were additional details on the following topics: ABC. We are a bit pressed for time now, so I'll have colleague D lead on this. While supporting colleague D, reference the information provided in the documents from the last quarter and speak with XYZ colleagues, if you need additional support. As this cannot be submitted for tomorrow's deadline, let's quickly brainstorm how to produce a fast turnaround.

There are hundreds of ways to approach similar problems of addressing difficult conversations like poor performance. Each situation may differ, but there are still methods that work **across the board**. If you are a non-native English speaker who is in a position of authority, be mindful of the fact that using insults to inspire motivation **seldom** works, if ever. In order to procure a positive outcome, keep your words neutral in tone and **stick to the facts**.

On the other hand, if you are a non-native English speaker who is working in a junior role, try addressing challenges and compromising situations with Passive Voice construction. (You will see how and when to form the Passive Voice in the next section, On Indirect Language). That being said, If it becomes necessary to defend yourself, switch to Active Voice and avoid using YOU, WHAT, and WANT.

Lastly, for people of color who are still marginalized and measured by the legacy of discrimination and stereotypes, it is **crucial** to remain professional. Even when **breaking away from** professionalism seems worthwhile, the resulting damage will only endanger your career while leaving your bigot's future unharmed, unaltered, and (at the worst of times) advanced. Protect yourself. Remain professional! I know it's hard, particularly when sweet visions of ripping apart your agitator comfort the wound. Pause (I'm terrible at this), discreetly count your breathing, and moderate your response. Stick to the facts and only the facts. Eliminate emotional vocabulary. Keep documents, leave a paper trail, and use email whenever possible. Develop an infallible record-keeping system. Trust your instincts. And never ever break professionalism.

LANGUAGE REVIEW

In ACTIVE VOICE, the main verb in the sentence is performed by the subject of the sentence. Often, the main verb follows directly behind the subject of the sentence. The pairing is commonly placed at the front of a sentence.

A nod is as good as a wink to a blind horse.

INDIRECT LANGUAGE

As stated in the last section, YOU is the most **precarious** word in *The Encyclopedia of Professional Communication*. When used carelessly, YOU has the distinctive power of immediately rebranding reputations as aggressive, defensive, overly-sensitive, and judgmental. A colleague's personality may be seen as overbearing, harassing, and chastising when he or she uses the pronoun YOU.

Why does this happen?

To recap, there is no direct translation for YOU when perceived in the plural form of a foreign tongue. In other words, the English language does not have a Second-Person Plural form—the form in other languages that is reserved for showing respect and formality. YOU in the English language is the Second-Person Singular form. While it may be used in both formal and informal contexts, it is undeniably direct language because it always identifies the action of a specific person. Funnily enough, the lack of ambiguity as to whom is being addressed or questioned immediately **wags a finger** in an accusing manner.

WHAT and WANT may not be personal pronouns but, colloquially, both words are often received abruptly. As I detailed in the last section, WHAT and WANT are aggressive and demanding when used as the main verb or paired next to a personal pronoun. Therefore, your inquiries and statements must artfully reconstruct the phrases in order to become passive and indirect.

The art of effective indirect language requires what I believe is a full command of the English language. In order to avoid being typecast as a challenging colleague during difficult times, your professional communication must become as **inventive** and **persuasive** as ever. You must answer the question: How can I address a colleague's actions (or seemingly worse, question a colleague's behavior), without saying YOU? Which phrases can I use in order to get what I want without using the word WANT? Do I really need to say, "Sorry, I didn't quite catch that," every time I need to say WHAT?

Yes, especially if you are a minority working in a hostile environment. Working in **the belly of the beast** is far from **child's play**. If you work in a bloodthirsty, warmongering, and hostile work environment, then **minding your Ps and Qs** is a matter of corporate survival. When protecting one's source of financial security is at stake, colleagues transform into career opportunists. We all have seen or heard about career opportunists who manipulate collegial environments in order to obtain a promotion or favoritism. We all have watched the gross misrepresentation of actions and comments made by vulnerable colleagues in order to protect or justify an outranking colleague's prejudices, insecurities, and discriminations. We all have been exposed to horror stories about the nature of failing HR interventions, which prolongs the culture of silencing victims and protecting their offenders. When these actions happen, the normalization of toxic behaviors cultivates the **abuse of power**. Moreover, if you are a person of color or a member of a protected class, I believe the stakes are higher for being strategically misrepresented and victimized by career opportunists. Time and time again, **at the end of this line**, employee disputes against HR offenders rarely **have their day in court**. You must learn how to protect yourself. You must master the art of professional communication!

PASSIVE VOICE

A wise formula that will always maintain indirect language is to eliminate YOU, WHAT, and WANT from your professional communication while using Passive Voice. This strategy will help you remain formal and indirect. As Passive Voice is not suitable for all situations, I suggest familiarizing yourself with its strengths and weaknesses. Perhaps the best way to understand when to use Passive Voice is to first understand its construction, and then learn how its construction impacts the meaning of each sentence.

Let's begin.

Firstly, Passive Voice differs from Active Voice because the subject of the sentence becomes the object of the sentence and vice versa. In other words, the order of the basic elements of a sentence changes! So, in order to understand the difference between Passive Voice construction and Active Voice construction better, you must remember the basic elements of a sentence: the subject, the verb, and the object.

The order of the basic elements of a sentence matters! The subject usually comes first (before the verb) and the object usually comes last (after the verb). Visually, this creates a pattern that I always refer to as SVO or SUBJECT-VERB-OBJECT.

For all intents and purposes of guiding you through sentence constructions, SVO sentence construction is called Active Voice. This sentence construction is Active Voice because the subject of the sentence is performing the action of the verb. In other words, whoever performs the action is the subject of the sentence; whomever (or whatever) receives the action is the object of the sentence. So, in Active Voice construction, the subject of the sentence is always followed by the main verb of the sentence.

Because the subject of the sentence is followed by the main verb in the sentence, there is no ambiguity as to whom is doing the verb. The lack of ambiguity helps form very clear and direct sentences (direct language). As such, SVO sentence construction is effective in top-down organizational structures. Decision-making authorities could truly earn the respect from their colleagues if they engage collegial environments by using Active Voice diplomatically. Ranking officers would delegate tasks and structure operational systems more easily when speaking and writing in Active Voice. Junior-level colleagues should consider clarifying objectives in Active Voice in order to proactively show how they aim to take responsibility for new projects. Regardless of the position, Active Voice is the go-to construction to use as you display pride in your work, provide guidance to others, and show respect for the dignity of your colleagues.

Empowering as Active Voice may be, there are times when I believe it's wiser to switch to Passive Voice. The decision to switch is based on situations, such as addressing poor performance or resolving minor conflicts. In order to understand why Passive Voice is ideal for these situations, you must first understand its construction.

When you are constructing Passive Voice, the object of the sentence comes first (before the past/present/future tense form of the verb) and the subject comes last (after the past/present/future tense form of the verb). Now, the object of the sentence appears as though it is the subject of the sentence, while the subject of the sentence appears as though it is the object of the sentence.

Let's take a look at an example.

I wrote the report.

Subject + Verb + Object
(ACTIVE VOICE)

The report was written by me.

Object + Verb + Subject
(PASSIVE VOICE)

The difference between Active Voice and Passive Voice is about answering the question: Who performs the action and to whom receives the action? In Passive Voice construction, to whom the action is received is emphasized because it comes first in the sentence. In Active Voice construction, who performs the action is emphasized because it comes first in the sentence. Therefore, Passive Voice always highlights the results of an action rather than spotlights whoever has done the action.

Because Passive Voice construction places greater attention on the action performed, using the construction becomes highly effective when addressing difficult situations in which no particular offender—or multiple colleagues—are at fault. In Passive Voice construction, you can focus all the attention on what was wrong rather than who was wrong.

You can discuss problematic results and choices made at great length without ever needing to isolate a group or individual. You can directly address how to resolve a situation while preserving the dignity of the wrongdoer, especially if you absolutely must address the wrongdoer publicly or among other colleagues. Essentially, when Passive Voice is used effectively, it is an excellent language device to use in order to maintain healthy work relationships **when the going gets tough.**

WHEN TO USE PASSIVE VOICE EFFECTIVELY

When there is no clear offender in a workplace conflict

When several colleagues have contributed to poor performance

To show a conscientious effort to achieve results

To show a commitment to face problems instead of **debasing** colleagues

To show a commitment to resolving issues as a team

The common thread in the different scenarios where Passive Voice becomes effective is indirectly addressing members of a team or a large group of people. Although there are many ways to be indirect, Passive Voice guarantees that the communication is focused on the action and not the person. As such, speaking in Passive Voice may even be suitable when you wish to acknowledge the achievements of a team or group; the effect of using this language device may be more inclusive and humbling.

But remember, **neither** Passive Voice **nor** Active Voice are tenses; they are tones. Therefore, each of the 12 tenses of the English language has its own form of the Passive Voice. Grammatically, Passive Voice is formed by referencing the object of the sentence first, followed by the past/present/future verb forms (tenses), followed by the Past Participle form of a verb.

The Tense Map below outlines how to form Passive Voice in all 12 tenses. **Take note** that both tenses of the Perfect Aspect have one Passive Voice form.

TENSE MAP
PASSIVE VOICE IN 12 TENSES
[OBJECT + PAST / PRESENT / FUTURE + PAST PARTICIPLE]

PAST SIMPLE The report was written	**PRESENT SIMPLE** The report is written	**FUTURE SIMPLE*** The report will be written
PAST CONTINUOUS The report was being written	**PRESENT CONTINUOUS** The report is being written	**FUTURE CONTINUOUS** The report will be being written
PAST PERFECT SIMPLE The report had been written	**PRESENT PERFECT SIMPLE** The report has been written	**FUTURE PERFECT SIMPLE** The report will have been written
PAST PERFECT CONTINUOUS The report had been being written	**PRESENT PERFECT CONTINUOUS** The report has been being written	**FUTURE PERFECT CONTINUOUS** The report will have been being written

*Consult the Language Review at the end of the section for more information about the Future Tense.

In conclusion, for the majority of the situations that you encounter, I encourage you to use a mixture of both Active Voice and Passive Voice in order to form formal and indirect language to inspire your colleagues or to address performance issues, respectively. Whenever you must address concerns in the Second Person, use indirect language as much as possible by switching to Passive Voice or use more inclusive pronouns like WE, US, and OUR. Lastly, for times when you must provide criticism or challenge a colleague, try to adhere to Passive Voice construction. In the beginning, your writing and speaking may feel robotic and perfunctory. As you develop your style as a professional communicator, explore how to use **artistic licenses** in order to become more approachable and welcoming with your formal and indirect dialogue.

LANGUAGE REVIEW

In ACTIVE VOICE, the main verb in the sentence is performed by the subject of the sentence.

In PASSIVE VOICE, the main verb in the sentence is performed by the object of the sentence.

*FUTURE SIMPLE: Remember, the Future Tense is, in fact, composed of the past and present tense forms using the modal WILL. In Future Simple, the forms of "THE SUBJECT+ WILL + VERB" and "THE SUBJECT+ AM GOING TO + VERB" are nearly equivalent in meaning. The nuance between the two forms expresses spontaneous decision-making versus pre-planned decision-making, respectively.

PART TWO

HOW TO, FROM A TEA SOMMELIER

THREE BASIC TYPES OF COMMUNICATIONS

A true command of the English language allows you to mix and match the four tonal categories for professional communication with ease. By strategically using any combination of the categorical ingredients from *Part One*, you can minimize communication breakdowns between you and your **target audience**. Aim for mastery of using each tonal category and the agility to move between them to improve your response time in both written and oral communication. I urge you to master this ability because strategic communication often requires adapting your communication style according to the demographics of your target audience. For instance, at an international conference on the links between Climate Change and Extreme Poverty, high-level representatives from Member States attend on behalf of their country. Panelists would be unwise to address attendees with informal and indirect language (and certainly not informal and direct language). This tonal combination might come across as lacking seriousness for the gravity of the theme at hand. Instead, formal and indirect language would be more appropriate. One might even consider a mixture of formal and informal language to connect with and persuade the target audience.

After the conference concludes, the same attendees will return home. Home-based meetings with either internal colleagues or via international conference calls generally tend to be more relaxed. Here, informal and indirect language for discussions and presentations might help move the conversation towards a more enjoyable experience.

True mastery of the tonal categories gives you the power to wield negotiations, presentations, settlements, and everyday speech in your favor. The effect is mesmerizing—a truly formidable and humbling experience.

When I started my **private practice** on the side as a consultant on Strategic Communications, I recognized many mistakes made by non-native English speakers—particularly in professional communication. Apart from grammatical errors, I believe most of the mistakes non-native English speakers make are tonal. These mistakes reflect errors that occur when translating directly from one's mother tongue into a foreign language. As detailed in *Part One*, the greatest danger in relying on direct translations is unintentionally sounding informal and direct when you meant to sound formal and indirect! By studying *Part One*, you can approach the work environment more strategically, especially when you must address uncomfortable situations or conflicts confidently without being unprofessional.

Remember, effective professional communication is about appealing to your audience's comfort zone. Moreover, strategic communication not only appeals to your target audience but also persuades them to adopt your vision, accept your suggestions, and respect your boundaries. Communication is the ultimate skill to master to build and maintain professional relationships. Therefore, study the tonal categories outlined in *Part One*. Each section of *Part One* contains the best recipe I have used and have seen in the professional world at the international level, which is the highest level of professional functionality.

Now, we move on to *Part Two: How To, from a Tea Sommelier.* In this section of the guidebook, we will move away from theoretical applications of tones (and voices) and delve into practical applications of professional and strategic communication. Let's begin!

Communication aims to resolve three basic issues:

When you WANT information.

When you need to PROVIDE information.

CONTRACTS and MONEY MATTERS.

Using what you have learned from *Part One*, approach each issue by keeping in mind one thought: How will my communication build effective professional relationships while addressing the issue at hand? As you read through the three basic types of communication in the following pages, remember, there are no hard rules on how to address or resolve them. I urge you to use the following pages as templates. They contain formats and proven strategies I've used to obtain fast results and provide quality satisfaction to clients and colleagues across the English-speaking world.

GRAMMATICALLY ACCURATE CULTURALLY AWKWARD

Lastly, as non-native English speakers, remember I also encourage you to follow by example first before using artistic license in oral communication. Live amongst an English-speaking environment before immediately trying to use creative, poetic, or new informal language. Always double-check with three to five different people to ensure that your informal language is culturally acceptable and appropriate for the situation or environment. Your grammar may be perfect with accurately formed long sentences, but if the wording is too colorful or misused, the reception will be awkward. Until you are confident in speaking fluidly, stick to formal language. Initially, the examples in *Part Two* may feel robotic and perfunctory. Over time, I am confident you will find your voice in a communication style that works well for you.

You catch more flies with honey than vinegar.

WHEN YOU WANT SOMETHING

Whether you are an entrepreneur or an employee, the main duty of any job is to obtain the results you want. In order to achieve results, job positions seek candidates who skillfully and diplomatically acquire what they need to secure a fast **turnaround**. In a word: resourcefulness; it's a top career skill. One way to build it in your professional communication relates to this chapter's proverb.

An old adage in the English language says, **"You catch more flies with honey than with vinegar."** This expression means it is better to use charming and soft-spoken language rather than aggressive or discourteous language in order to get what you want. In professional English-speaking environments, I advise all professionals to use a combination of formal and indirect language when making requests. As we have already learned from *Part One*, in English-speaking cultures, using polite modals will soften the reception of your request. And constructing passive voice sentences with polite modals will dispel any notion of **putting the receiver on the spot.**

STEP 1

Modify your **salutation**. Begin with a salutation that reflects the relationship dynamic between you and the recipient, as well as the situation you are about to discuss. (For suggestions on formal and indirect salutations in English, refer to *The Encyclopedia of Professional Communication* at the end of the book in the appendix).

STEP 2

Always begin with a positive statement. Always! Granted, this step usually brings about amusing, mixed reactions from my clients. I suggest this step because, in fast-paced environments where jobs require you to transform into machines, a common complaint from colleagues is feeling overlooked, dismissed, and unappreciated. So, showing collegial interest in your colleague is a small gesture that **goes a long way**. My go-to statement when I can't really think of anything clever to say is, "I hope this message finds you well."

STEP 3

State your needs and be sure to be very clear. Remember from the section, On Formal Language, that using the polite form of modals instantly softens your language. Be **brief**. Use one to two sentences and keep them short. And also remember to be confident by taking the initiative; this means, construct your request by using polite modals and stating exactly what you would like to see as the result. This strategy has had a high rate of positive acceptance in my career, and now I **bequeath** it to you.

STEP 4

Provide several details after you have stated your request, if need be. Remember, this is a work environment, and most email readers do not have time to read an essay. Use **brevity** as much as possible. Ten-worded sentences are easy to **digest**. Furthermore, colleagues are conducting more and more business via digital devices, so be concise and kind with the reading length on tiny screens.

STEP 5

End your request by gently suggesting when you would like the information. The keyword here is "gently". Lastly, I would also suggest you use indirect language to passively say you'll follow up shortly.

Applying the steps above to situations that require **seeking out** information or getting something you need or want. As there is something you want and don't have, you are the one who is at a professional disadvantage. So be gentle with modal-back language. I have found that using this formula above secures the fastest results with the least amount of correspondence.

Now it's your turn.

Use the following pages below to draft practice emails. Ask a native English-speaking professional to review your draft for accuracy in grammar, clarity, and tone. Keep this guidebook as a reference for future emails and oral exchanges until you've mastered the technique and have found your own effective style.

TO REQUEST A MEETING

1. Salutations are subtle yet strongly suggestive; they set the tone of the rest of your message. Choose wisely.	Hello[1] Hana,
2. This positive opener is an excellent way to maintain a strong professional relationship. Acknowledge that your colleague is more than an operating system!	It was lovely that we could catch up at the event last Thursday.[2]
3. Remember, no one at work has time for a sermon. Immediately after your positive opener, state the reason for the email. Put it in a nutshell.	I got to thinking about our conversation on creating a training course to strengthen capacity-building measures in WASH programs for healthcare leaders in the LDCs.[3]
4. Requests are more readily received with softer language. Use polite modals instead of saying, "We can" and "How does". The devil is in the details!	Perhaps we could find a way to bring this to fruition if we joined forces? How does a partnership sound between your office and my team to build and advertise this course?[4]
5. Notice how this email has been drafted without using the word "YOU". Relying on "WE", "OUR", and "US" makes professional communication feel more inclusive, which lessens the feeling of being put on the spot.	If this sounds interesting and beneficial, then perhaps we[5] could discuss this over lunch? May I gently propose meeting on Thursday, June 28th, at 13:15 at Peekbone?[6] Please feel free to suggest another location and time that is more convenient for your diary.[7]
6. Using modals, gently state exactly what you want from your addressee. Understand that this strategy allows the recipient to reject your proposal, but most often, an acceptance is on the way back to you.	
7. This sentence is a stylistic strategy. It further underlines the requesting colleague's willingness to be accommodating and flexible.	I look forward to hearing your thoughts soon.[8]
8. Conclusions can be used wisely to passively suggest you will be following up shortly.	Well wishes,[9] Ilya
9. Similar to salutations, valedictions can also vary in tone. Select the best complimentary close.	

The tone in this email is obviously very light and friendly, yet professional and courteous. The tone is set from the beginning, where Ilya addresses Hana with an informal salutation. Clearly, Ilya and Hana have not only met more than once but also share a professional relationship that is **on an equal footing**—maybe even genuinely friendly. Choosing "hello" instead of "dear" may be more effective in building a strong professional relationship because the latter is the most formal out of all the salutations in the English language. Strong formalities often create and sustain a chasm in building working relationships.

Salutations are often taken for granted. I believe salutations are important as they set the tone for the entire email; they immediately intimate the type of relationship between the writer and receiver. Oh, the pain of learning how to use salutations accurately and strategically! Funnily enough, when I began to work in team-oriented positions at the international level, there were countless times I used the wrong salutation. Professional growing pains. Rookie mistakes.

My all-time favorite communication strategy to address when I want something from a colleague or client is expressed in subscript six. Gently planting seeds to move requests forward significantly reduces email correspondence, thereby speeding up productivity. At first glance, the notion of proposing your preferences may seem too forward. I hear you. Take comfort in remembering you are in a professional, fast-paced working environment. This is business! For this reason, crafting your proposal with modals and indirect language gives the receiver the understanding that the request can be altered, **postponed**, or dismissed entirely. The request becomes just a suggestion... just another option... just another possibility to consider. Your receiver should feel in control of your proposal— even though the proposal is coming from you. But in actuality, you remain in control because you planted the seed and provided a fully thought-out plan. More often than not, your kind and gentle request will be accepted or slightly adapted. I dare you to try it. I dare you to love it.

Leave of absence requests are likely one of the most controversial workplace scenarios. Ideally, I agree with Human Resource professionals who advise making such a request in person directly to your manager. However, our world is entrenched in employment discrimination, so I

REQUEST AN URGENT LEAVE OF ABSENCE

Dear Doha,	1. Remember, choose your salutations wisely, particularly as you are in need of something quite serious and urgent. Set the tone.
I hope this email finds you well.	
Recently, extenuating circumstances outside of work have arisen for me over the last few days. I have been trying to juggle my work responsibilities while addressing this personal concern, but with great difficulty.	2. Consider using some variation of this phrase when you are at a loss for words regarding a positive opener.
	3. Depending on the relationship you have with your manager, consider being as specific as possible without compromising your privacy.
As we are wrapping up our software installation project with Mirakios Co. this week, may I please request a leave of absence for 1-2 days sometime next week? If acceptable, I would be happy to prepare Vanessa to provide cover and will keep my mobile with me for added assurance.	4. As leave of absences are quite serious in tone, ideally, managers are appreciative when there is ample notice in advance. For urgent requests (as per this example), it may be helpful to show how you are considering the workload of your team, manager, and the impact of your absence.
I would be grateful to take leave on Monday and Tuesday; however, I am happy to work around team priorities should other days be more suitable.	5. Offer flexibility with the days you are requesting, if possible. Otherwise, be highly mindful of the impression extended weekends may give off.
Best, Gregory	
	6. Refer to the list of valedictions in the appendix.

also believe it is wise to document the request by email. Regarding the proper way to request a leave of absence, undoubtedly each country and institution has its own laws or policies, respectively. Therefore, I encourage all employees to become familiar with their workplace's procedures and policies **on taking leave**. This is particularly necessary for scenarios in which there are no legal protections, as there would be for medical concerns, civic duties, maternity, or paternity statuses, etc.

Let's look at some dynamics in one of the latest cultural paradigm shifts, which could impact a leave of absence request. Picture a scenario in which a colleague asks for a leave of absence for a "mental health day".

In my country, the stigma behind mental health issues is exponentially changing. I believe the change is due to open dialogues held at the national and local level with leaders and role models in the media industry who have helped combat misinformation proliferated by Hollywood-like portrayals of mental health and mental illnesses. Conversely, outside the protection of fame, fortune, and followers, expressing mental health challenges still recalls powerful imagery of emotionally and cognitively unstable victims. I have seen how the notion of an emotionally or mentally unstable colleague will not only scar a colleague's reputation but will also call into question a colleague's performance fitness at any future time when the slightest bit of anxiety, stress, or exhaustion is displayed.

We all know that life happens, yet collegial environments' receptivity to the term "mental health" wavers, if not entirely disappears. For this reason, I do not believe we have matured at either the national or international level on mental health issues. I do believe, as a global society, we are aiming to get there. Until we do, expressing concerns for your mental health at work often is immediately interpreted as suffering mental illness. Mental health is of paramount importance and is part of one's first point of defense against burnout and defeat. You must protect your mental health! **Period**.

As workplace environments have a history of shamefully discounting colleagues who raise mental health concerns, I will not encourage anyone to openly express their mental health journey— especially if you are without a protective financial platform designed to secure your bread and butter (i.e., Hollywood), should your truth be weaponized against you. While I will not encourage anyone to put their job at risk, I will support those who selflessly put their job at risk for the benefit and advancement of society. In both scenarios, bravery can be found.

Moving deeper into reporting mental health issues at work, I am concerned for people of color and members of protected classes who openly reveal they are in need of a day to protect their health. I deeply fear that their choice to be honorably transparent may lead to a time when they are prohibited from accelerating in their **post** due to spiteful colleagues' whispered concerns of their "perceived" mental state. Comments similar to the following are doomed to surface:

> "Oh, remember what happened to Mark last year around this time? I heard from John that he was asking for some sick days, but he wasn't ill. He just didn't want to be at work, I reckon. Maybe this upcoming project might be a bit... I don't know...too much. Don't you think? Let's find someone more reliable to do it."

"I heard that three months ago, Anna took a leave of absence. I think it had something to do with her brother… I don't know. One of her managers was talking about it on the way to work. Maybe we should find another team member to lead on this project. It's too highly visible for something to go wrong."

Gossip has a powerfully corrosive nature to hang prey by unverified comments and actions at their predator's bidding. Without even consulting with you, your "collegial enemies" have no problem sowing doubt about your performance abilities if it will help to discredit your integrity or deter you from career advancement. Lesson to be learnt: words matter.

Moving deeper into this issue, I strongly advise people of color and members of protected classes to be wise when requesting a leave of absence. Yes, arguably, gossip similar to those above can easily apply to any colleague in a work environment, regardless of his or her background. Sadly, however, in toxic environments replete with a history of bullying, harassment, and discrimination, I have seen these damning comments work against people of color and members of protected classes disproportionately higher. So, if you are a person of color or a member of a protected class, comments like the above are further impregnated with all the stereotypes associated with your minority status. Please do not put yourself **in the lion's den** by needlessly disclosing private information. Learn exactly what you must disclose by becoming aware of your workplace's hiring policies and equal opportunity laws for the country that hired you.

Lastly, if you really believe that racism, sexism, and all other discriminatory "-isms" are extinct or don't really exist, then **take the bait** and **bear your soul** to your employer or boss. Be prepared for the oncoming result or consequences, especially if you are a person of color.

As we try to climb the career ladder, life seems predestined to fight against us. Engaging in flexible work schemes is an excellent way to address personal or private concerns while maximizing your performance at work. However, a flexible work request may raise similar concerns as a request for a leave of absence. Therefore, take similar precautions regarding the formation of your request.

REQUEST FLEXIBLE WORKING HOURS

1. In your request for flexible work, tie in your proposal how the new work arrangement will add value to your job responsibilities.	Dear Valeriya, I would be grateful to have your approval on new aims[1] for my objectives this fall.
2. One of the best justifications for flexible working hours is how they can enhance your professional development. Look for justifications that will ultimately benefit your company or organization once the request is approved.	As part of the office's new Learning and Development program, I would be grateful to take advantage of their L&D Reimbursement Programme.[2]
3. Include a proposal that focuses on the added value to the team, your manager, and/or the company or organization at large.	I wanted to discuss possible ways I may include this into my performance objectives for this year. Attached is my proposal, which details how the certification will improve my work performance
4. There are times when I've seen or received correspondences without a traditional valediction. In general, these letters have varied in tone from positive to neutral to aggressive. As stated before, choose your complimentary closing wisely. I advise that if you choose to forego the tradition, ensure the tone of your message is positive and light.	as well as open new opportunities to help the company expand.[3] I've also included a provisional schedule that sets aside 5 hours per week at the city center's training institute, which is quite close to our office. Many thanks in advance for the consideration. Elena[4]

Overall, I've seen formal and indirect language as the most effective approach to ensure results are obtained when making requests. This approach helps maintain collegial relationships while protecting your credibility and respectability on the job. Arguably, there are cons to this approach; professional etiquette to this degree can often feel perfunctory and lies in danger of seeming insincere and repetitive. So, your goal is to practice sociable adaptations in addition to formal and indirect communication to naturalize responses.

And remember, "WANT" is one of the three most damning words in You simply cannot say, "I want…" when you are dependent on another colleague or stakeholder.

Less is more.

WHEN YOU MUST PROVIDE INFORMATION

By far, informative emails and similar forms of correspondence are hopefully the easiest forms of communication for you. Sometimes, however, in our quest to appear knowledgeable, we may overlook email etiquette in addition to the tone set by our use of English. I would encourage you to keep informative emails concise and rely heavily on email attachments. "Less is more" really defines the collegial philosophy behind constructing excellent need-to-know emails.

As we have already learned from the very beginning of the guidebook, brevity in English-speaking etiquette lies in danger of being perceived as discourteous. Therefore, using polite modals is still a good strategic communication approach as you form shorter communiqués. While you use polite modals, lean on informal and indirect language to share information with colleagues and clients. I say this because, in your informative emails, you are not at a disadvantage when you provide information to the recipient of the email. You are only at a disadvantage when you *want* something from the recipient. (Refer to the guidance in the previous section). Still, using styles of formality never hurts when used strategically. In other words: be charming. To that end, using polite modals with informal and indirect language feels more lighthearted and approachable in tone than strictly using formal language. Have fun with your phrasal verbs and idioms! Just ensure that they have been selected wisely and are in step with professional etiquette in English.

Consider the tips below on how to construct pithy yet approachable, informative emails. These steps should help you **garner** a reputation for sending worthwhile emails that colleagues appreciate opening.

STEP 1

As always, pick a salutation suitable for the body of your email. Unless the announcement is quite serious in tone, I would refrain from using "Dear colleagues" as your salutation. Let's face it: informative emails are usually skimmed, if even opened. So encourage your colleagues to read beyond the salutation. Try "Greetings" or "Hello all" or "Welcome Carla".

STEP 2

In one sentence, state as succinctly as possible why you have just asked your very busy and impatient colleague to open your email. Use as much positive language as possible. A rule of thumb: if you cannot summarize the purpose of the informative email in one short 10-15 worded sentence (or less), then it most likely should not be sent. This may hurt, but in the age of digital communication, no one has time to read an essay.

STEP 3

Out of all the steps listed, I wholeheartedly believe the most important is to rely heavily on attachments. This way, the body of your email remains short and easily digestible. Unless a senior recipient requests for the information to be placed in the body of the email, use attachments generously.

STEP 4

Further to Step 3, pull pertinent information from the attachments to highlight in the body of the email. This may include significant comments, calls for action, policy-changing content, etc. Keep it short and simple.

STEP 5

Surely this should go without saying: as you are the provider of the informative email, kindly leave a happy line on how to follow up with you directly for more information. If you truly are not the right person with whom to follow up, then leave **a gentle nod in the right direction**.

INTERNAL COMMUNICATIONS (SERIOUS)

1. In this correspondence, the sender is providing information that is still serious in tone. Formality is best.	Dear colleagues,[1] As you're probably aware, there will be a system-wide shutdown on the network starting Thursday, March 14th at 18:59 GMT.[2] It's expected to last throughout the weekend and should end at 23:59 on Sunday, March 17th.[3]
2. Because the tone is serious, one communication tactic is to simply get to the main point as fast as possible.	
3. Notice how this section uses a mixture of formal language and informal language. It uses a polite modal and also contractions. The latter is often regarded as informal language.	As such, we[4] need to organize ourselves as best we can in advance. Please kindly refer to the guidance attached for entering into and exiting out of the building with your security pass. If you[5] have any trouble, kindly reach us by phone at +1 555 876 3647.
4. For informal and indirect communiqués, rely on inclusive language as much as possible. Use "we," "us," and "our" instead of directly addressing the recipient.	
5. As there is a point of action for the recipient in a serious-toned email, use hot words like "YOU" minimally and in a positive statement.	Many thanks and have a lovely weekend.[6] Antonina Head of DMTR Security Team
6. Notice here that the complimentary close serves as the valediction. This gives the email a more serious tone in nature.	

INTERNAL COMMUNICATIONS (LIGHT-HEARTED)

Greetings all,[1]	1. This salutation is very lighthearted and immediately sets the tone for the rest of the positive and uplifting email.
I wish you and your family well during these uncertain times.[2]	2. The opening statement makes an effort to acknowledge that colleagues are more than operating systems or soulless. By extending hope for good health to colleagues' families, a personal and empathic touch helps move eyes down a bit further.
I am very pleased to announce that our partnership with Drolas Inc. has taken effect. Starting in two weeks' time, we will launch the new campaign on children's literacy with Spring Octave LTD.[3]	
	3. Don't dawdle with your main point. State it as soon as possible in detailed and brief sentences.
This venture could not have been possible without the committed work from the Sales and Marketing team.[4]	4. Notice how Passive Voice is used both here and in superscript 6. The construction more strongly highlights the positive outcome by placing the result in the front of the sentence, rather than placing who or what brought about the result first. Receiving the venture and the "Thank you" note is more important than who performed the actions. Therefore, the object comes first.
To see some early results of their successes, I've attached snapshots of their program thus far.[5] A generous "Thank You" note has also been included, which was signed directly by the VP of Spring Octave.[6]	
	5. Rely on attachments, and your colleagues will thank you.
	6. Ibid 4.
Well done to Sales and Marketing for opening this new door.[7] I look forward to hearing more about the progress ahead.[8]	7. Compare this sentence in Active Voice to the Passive Voice sentences above. Congratulating the subject, "Sales and Marketing," is more important than the act of opening a new door. Therefore, the subject comes first.
	8. Politely signal your expectations by using the phrase, "I look forward to..." This can also serve effectively as a call to action for your recipients.
Well wishes to all,[9] Carla	9. The valediction, (also known as a "complimentary close") is well-balanced in tone with the positive email. It is still professional yet not severely formal.

EXTERNAL COMMUNICATIONS (MAINTAINING RELATIONSHIPS)

1. In external emails, this approach is a traditional yet common way to formally address those of heightened importance. It is flattering, as it relies on identifying the recipient with a distinguished title. The body of this email is one to study. It has been formed using a mixture of formal and informal language. The salutation helped to mark the tone of the email as a formal yet inviting letter. Clearly, it has been written to help maintain ties and continue building a healthy professional relationship with the recipients. Notice there is an absence of hot words and a reliance on inclusive pronouns. Sentences are drafted longer too. With the inclusion of modals and several popular expressions, the formal and informal language aids the indirect tone well.

2. To end this informative letter, the drafter used a valediction that is soft and very respectful. It reinforces his commitment to servicing the recipient to whom it was sent.

To our Esteemed Panelists,

On behalf of the Public Affairs and Client Relations team, I would like to take this opportunity to say thank you for your participation in our regional conference.

The insight each of you has provided on the new trends of sustainable wind energy and its impact on the local population has brought a new challenge to our table that will not go unaddressed.

We are committed to renewing the ongoing relationship and engagement with the local community to ensure their futures are secured by changing our environmental policies and practices. Ensuring the local community has full access to participate in the discussion remains a top priority.

Thank you once again for your powerful messages. We hope to follow up with you all in the upcoming weeks ahead.

Humbly yours,
Frank

PERFECT CHEMIS-TEA

EXCEPTIONS TO THE RULES

Oh, yes. As language learners, we know that rules in all languages have exceptions. One noticeable exception to informative emails written in English is choosing whether to use Active or Passive Voice. In order to engage your readers from the beginning, Active Voice immediately draws in your target audience. Although Active Voice is a direct form of communication, pacifying the tone with polite modals and positive content will help move the communication from a direct tone to an indirect one.

Another considerable exception is based on the decision to use the inflammatory words YOU, WHAT, and WANT in informative emails. What do you want to convey in tone? Again, when used alongside wholehearted, positive messaging, the tone of the email is less accusatory and confrontational. So the use of YOU, WHAT, and WANT becomes more personable in tone and brings forth lively colorful language, which creates a more enjoyable read. From what I've seen, the most effective use of hot words is in campaigning emails. I use the word "campaigning" as broadly as explicitly possible.

The last area to consider for exceptions to the rules is oral presentations. Tangentially, I call attention to oral presentations because effective and engaging public speaking requires a balance between all four tonal categories of professional communication and the active and strategic use of the hot words YOU, WHAT, and WANT. Furthermore, giving a presentation in a foreign tongue is a challenge **of its own**. Among having to think in a new language system—especially when fluency has yet to be achieved—there are other factors at play that make or break a presentation aimed at successfully providing information. The following is a comprehensive list of oral presentation flaws doomed to prey on presenters regardless of English-speaking fluency levels.

A LACK OF DIRECTION

Perhaps the greatest presentation flaw across the board is appearing to have a lack of direction or a lack of purpose. In a 45-minute presentation, viewers leave feeling as though they cannot get back the precious time they have just lost. Even if you had a purpose for your presentation, its worthiness becomes lost through poor organization, among other lacking skills. To avoid such destruction, I advise you **to boil down** your content to three key messages. The best way to do so is to ask yourself: what do you want the most senior member or influencer to take away from your speech? List the three most important overall main messages. This will become the purpose of your presentation and the justification behind your audience participation. Put it in a nutshell. To not lose focus, write each of the three key messages in 10-word sentences.

RAMBLING

Within each of the three overall key messages you would like to present, **get straight to the point**. Your presentation may now be focused, but your explanations may not be. Our insecurities like self-consciousness and self-doubt contribute to nervousness. A common symptom of nervousness while presenting is the unconscious behavior of **rambling** on and on. Therefore, to prevent rambling, identify three points of interest per each key message. Essentially, you are deconstructing each key message by repeating the strategy above. Now you have your points of interest clearly and simply stated. Be sure to briefly state how each point of interest would, could, or should impact your listener directly.

WAY TOO LONG

Unless you have a high-profile name, no one (and I do mean no one) wants to be held in a lecture-like business presentation. Rarely do I speak on behalf of the masses. And yet here, with full confidence, I reiterate that professional sermons are overrated, outdated, and a downright infringement on colleagues' time and schedules.

Undoubtedly, the previous two presentation flaws above contribute to unnecessarily lengthy presentations. However, if you have 45 minutes for a presentation, you need not use all 45 minutes presenting. Find creative ways to engage your audience. Otherwise, you are simply speaking to a human wall, a still sea, or worse still: a mirror.

Information overload is not a mark of intellectual prowess. Instead, it highlights and exposes a lack of confidence—plain and simple. Stick to the approach above to keep your key messages and points of interest succinct and pithy. By doing so, you'll find that wandering minds and glazed-over looks are at a minimum—if even present, due to your delivery of a short and high-impact presentation.

This strategy I find always brews the most enticing and seductively powerful cup of tea: soothing, flavorful, and all within the modest depth of a teacup. It puts the *Oh-là-là* in the pleasure of **feeding off** the palpability of one's words. With this mixture, your audience will want more.

Think of the most amazing selection of a truffle, a Michelin chef's greatest dish, or the slightest trace of your favorite scent. In all of these scenarios, a small portion is always given from a much greater and delightful treat. You must craft your presentation likewise in order to obtain a powerful, lasting, and memorable impact. Less truly is more.

Give as much-needed details as possible in a short timeframe. When I train clients, I always shoot for a 7-minute window for a presentation. 7-minute presentations have consistently proven to be the most impactful and memorable. If the time restriction is too great a challenge, then aim between 7-15 minutes in length to present content within a 45-minute structure.

The rest of the time should be used for **Q&A**, in which you can go into greater detail on points of interest as it concerns your audience. In this way, you have truly targeted your audience.

FORCED JOKES

Some speakers are natural comedians. If you are not one, a professional oral presentation is not the place to try out your latest comedic swag that is predestined to fail. Please don't try to be amusing. This advice sounds like a **no-brainer**. Yet, countless would-be jokesters underestimate the stigma of using poor taste in language, especially when trying to gain the favor of colleagues. The result is a lingering air of awkwardness and discomfort, with only the negative reviews worth remembering. Just stick to the facts and content of your presentation. As I wrote earlier in *Part One*, I truly do not know how to have a genuine personality at work in environments destined to swallow vulnerable social groups whole. So, exploring a comedic side whilst presenting to your clients and colleagues is not the best strategy towards climbing the career ladder.

POOR PRONUNCIATION

For non-native English speakers, my heart goes out to you when presenting in English. During my travels and work experience outside the United States, I've noticed how my poor speaking ability in foreign languages is received by locals. Comparatively, the experience often appears more welcoming than non-native English speakers being received by a native English-speaking audience. The native English-speaking community **on the whole** seems to still be evolving in regard to its welcomed receptivity of non-native English speakers.

As such, I encourage non-native English speakers to spend less time on perfecting grammar and more time on mastering keywords, terms, and phrases that are central to the comprehensiveness of their presentation. When I train clients for their upcoming presentation, I usually use the following strategy outlined below. In a 90-minute to 2-hour session, clients recite their presentation four to seven times. During the last two or three times, I track mispronounced words and sounds consistently missed by the client. These targeted words and sounds become the central focus in order to improve elocution.

So even if the client is at an intermediate speaking level in English, I am not concerned about grammar and tenses as much as I am about keywords, terms, and phrases that are central to the messaging of the presentation. One needs not to speak English perfectly to be understood. I mean, not even native English-speaking presenters speak English perfectly! Knowing this, rest assured you need not worry about how bad your grammar is nor how many words you don't know. If you have been assessed as speaking any foreign language at an intermediate level, you have proven that a general audience can understand you.

For English-speaking crowds, which may have low tolerance for less than perfect English, I strongly advise you to take your time when speaking in English. Practice only the words most essential to the meaning of your presentation and master their pronunciation and accent; these are the only words that must be mastered! Once you are comfortable pronouncing your target keywords, try presenting for a small team in your office. Focus on their face and body language. See how your mastery of keywords deepens and widens the comprehension pool of your target audience.

NO RHYTHM

Take a few moments now to search for the best speakers in history. Use Google, Yandex, or **whichever floats your boat**. I bet the one common thread uniting all powerful speakers appearing in your search engine is that each of them speaks slowly. Every notable figure in World History who has harnessed the power of oration speaks slowly and purposefully. This is not by accident; it is by choice and design.

I urge all oral communicators to slow down their pace of speech. Find a rhythm. You are designing a musical composition when you speak. You are composing a symphony of diction, syntax, and pitch when you speak. You are sculpting breath and molding sound into tangible form when you speak. In short, you are an artist (albeit a vocal artist), and words are your craft. Craft your words wisely! And share them slowly.

An unseeable rhythm forms with powerful orators. By its very nature, it can only be felt and not seen by human eyes. Lately, I've begun to wonder if the art of oral communication is more easily adaptable to kinesthetic learners whilst more challenging for highly visual learners.

A wordsmith becomes an orator upon mastering the art of sound. Furthermore, the art of oral communication is a beat; similar to proficient rappers, poets, truly unique singers and lyricists. These talented communicators have the power to bend the social fabric along a new trajectory in which results a new social history. Speaking is just another artistic form.

In English, the task may feel more daunting. One reason for the trepidation may be because the language is quite limited in its range of sultry vocabulary, in my opinion. In fact, no other foreign language have I studied thus far is more belligerent than the English language. The English language was born out of blood; it remains the bloodiest language I have ever studied in my life. If you have yet to research the thrilling, brutal history of the English language, I'll leave you to explore the war-torn grievances that birthed one of the bloodiest languages on Earth.

Perhaps skilled speakers of English know precisely how to counterbalance the harshness and rigidity of its character. And that is your goal as an oral communicator; transform the English language from mere informal and indirect prose into your metrical structure of oration.

STEP 1

Structure your presentation to last seven to fifteen minutes in a 45-minute time slot. Reserve the remaining minutes for Q&A and for going in-depth on topics of interest.

STEP 2

To structure your presentation, identify three overall key messages for your presentation. Write down each message in a 10-word sentence.

STEP 3

For each key message, find three points of interest. Again, write down each point of interest in a 10-word sentence.

STEP 4

Ensure that each point of interest expresses a specific takeaway for the audience.

STEP 5

Before ending, restate the three overall key messages and frame them in context as to how they will help or impact the lives of your audience. Then, **open the floor** for Q&A.

The love of money is the root of all evil.
1 Timothy 6:10

CONTRACTS AND MONEY MATTERS

Out of the four tonal categories of professional communication, direct language seems to be the tone that is most difficult to engage and use effectively. Furthermore, in today's world, I find that direct language is often wrongly defined and represented by many forms that are **flat out** unprofessional: cursing, swearing, pejoratives, insults, etc. This is not direct language; this is rude language! To label these behaviors as direct language weakens truly powerful and direct communication.

As written in *Part One*, direct language is the absence of polite modals. There are times when I find their absence a form of protection in my communication aims, particularly when negotiating contracts and managing money matters. However, remember from the disclaimer: I am not a lawyer and so cannot provide any legal counsel. Instead, I urge you to seek legal counsel the moment you suspect it is necessary.

So, in this short section, I express a choice decision that has helped me keep safe in toxic environments. Whenever I sniff a whiff of danger or precariousness, I immediately switch to formal in direct language. In both written and oral form, the tone is firm, refrains from rudeness and conveys strictly business. I share what I've learnt with the hope that my lesson may bring some additional insight when you face murky waters to keep you out of harm's way.

When I could not afford a lawyer and did not have access to friends with legal advice, I made sure to stick to formal and direct language only. Polite modals were absent and the careful constructing of sentences using YOU, WHAT, and (rarely) WANT were crafted with great care. All of my communication adhered strictly to facts. This meant that a statement of fact did not rely on adverbs nor adjectives. I quickly realized that the moment I chose to use any adverb or adjective in my communication, the power of direct communication was lost and my statement of fact was questionable or vulnerable. The veracity of adverb and adjective-infused statements moved out of the realm of facts and quickly into opinions. In other words, the language transformed into an emotional response. Opinions and feelings mean nothing to those who regulate policies, guidelines, and laws. As a minority and member of a protected class, protecting oneself in documented and written form is paramount; it must be done so with facts. So, unless I was directly quoting someone's words, I eliminated all forms of emotional vocabulary (adverbs and adjectives) in formal and direct correspondence. All communication was presented or followed up with a timestamped written report (email) of transpired events or discussions and agreements.

Formal and direct language left behind a strong and lingering reputation that I was a tough, no-nonsense colleague, client, or negotiator. The choice to switch into formal and direct language only when absolutely necessary saved my life. The strategic move contributed to the elevation of my career goals. I'm proud of my CV, especially as a young black woman from limited beginnings. My tailored professional approach has placed me in professional settings like the United Nations or training clients in distinguished international companies.

Prejudices, discriminatory language, racist and sexist behaviors, ageism and all other forms of bigotry are still haunting our daily interactions with few laws established to identify and prosecute such vilification. My advice to any professional **under the gun** of bigotry or in a toxic environment is to switch all communication to formal and direct language, and ensure all communication is documented in written form. For people of color and those who are members of a protected class, never use any emotional language in writing—ever! Track all of your communication in a timestamped, written form. Email is one of the best methods, though not always possible or advisable. Seek legal counsel whenever possible. Keep every document safe and stowed away at home. In hostile and toxic environments, minimize verbal exchanges at all costs or ensure you are surrounded by supportive peers, which is very difficult to maneuver. Remember, every professional looks out for himself or herself when securing one's bread and butter is at stake.

History is replete with examples of how bigots retain the majority vote, especially if they have been given a position of power. Bigots remain in power because they have support and laws to protect them. Bigots remain bigots because laws are written by bigots.

False friends are worse than open enemies.

A NOTE ON BUILDING WORKPLACE RELATIONSHIPS

To seek or not to seek personal relationships at work? That is the question. I'll address the answer through a personal story.

When I was growing up in America, my mother worked as a Registered Nurse. Years later, I learned that she had advanced to become the head of her department as the Floor Manager. I never had the impression that my mother liked her job; as many immigrants' stories go, it served more as a means to an end: a sacrificial process to ensure her daughters were properly educated in the United States.

My mother would often come home angry and upset about something that happened on the job. Rarely would she ever go into details or even mention the problems forthrightly. Instead, during the times when she thought she was alone, I would eavesdrop into her private renditions of heated scenes from the hospital. To watch her exasperation through a crack in the door was heartbreaking and puzzling. Many years later, when similar workplace struggles entered into my adult life, I came to understand introspective monologues were a coping mechanism to maintain self-empowerment and prepare the mind to resist offenders who were awaiting to attack the next day.

Until I had gained experience in the workforce, I tried to understand my mother's coping mechanism through the only juvenile process I had used up to then: friendships. Friendships were my coping mechanism. Friendships were my source of strength. During the tender years of my life, friendships kept me grounded whilst providing a wall of safety. So one evening, I approached my mother: "Mom, don't you have friends at work?" Without skipping a beat, she replied, "Your colleagues are your colleagues. They are not your friends."

Seventeen years of work experience has taught me that she was right. And not so right.

As a parting gift from a post at the United Nations, a colleague took me to dinner. There, for the first time, we had a heart-to-heart chat about our personal lives and experiences at work. I was a bit nervous to expose private details but rationalized that I would probably never want to work in the position again and I most likely would never see my colleague again, so I trusted my gut. She had a very calming presence and seemed genuinely happy to receive mine. She gave me a book to take on my travels and I left thinking: she's such a lovely person! How can I keep in touch with her when I'm gone?

A few weeks later, she organized a weekend beach trip in New Jersey with some like-minded communal colleagues who I had never really seen nor met at work. The five of us were similar in temperament, even though our lives and personalities were vastly different. As the years passed, we made an effort to keep in touch. Whilst I was in Russia, I kept thinking how my work-life balance would have been measurably different had I known these women whilst at work.

The opposite side of this spectrum relates to office romances. In an article I read years ago, listed were the three main ways significant others are found today outside online dating: at school, through a friend or at work. For the latter, workplace romances might unfold like a typical Rom-Com from a Hollywood film. However, if disaster strikes, the burden of engaging with your ex-partner may challenge professional credibility.

With the recent MeToo and Time's Up movements, I deeply believe flirtatious language and behavior at work is a honey trap. And yet, I have no solution or advice to offer to those who ask about pursuing romance in the workplace. Given my upbringing, I'm doubtful if I would ever promote or entertain the idea of finding a significant other at work. And yet, there are wonderful stories where budding office romances bloom colorfully and successfully inside the lion's den. Therefore, all I can say is to be very careful and intentional with your art of communication if someone pursues you with playful language. And as always, do my favorite phrase: err on the side of caution!

My bottom line comes down to this: I've seen colleagues engage without an ulterior motive to build effective and sometimes long-lasting relationships. On the other hand, I've seen colleagues take each other's personal lives, stories and sensitive information to use as a noose around their opponent's neck to hang them by it. The motivation for this behavior is always the same: to profit socially and/or economically at a colleague's expense for personal gain at work. For this reason, I find it difficult to build genuine friendships in the workspace, nevertheless romantic ones.

So, when romance is not the aim of workplace interactions, using effective professional communication to build strong professional relationships results in mutually profitable opportunities, exchanges, and deliverables.

A drop of ink may make a million think.

A soft answer turneth away wrath; but grievous words stir up anger.
Proverbs 15:1

THE PERFORMANCE REVIEW

Across the board, one of the most entertaining exercises I perform with my clients is drafting a performance review. Outside English-speaking cultures, the responses are always hilarious. It remains one of the best parts of my training course. Yes, it's very easy to rave about high-functioning performers who are exceptionally talented, productive and clever. However, what if you are cursed with a tenured poor performer? When you hire a new colleague who you feel works like a blockhead compared to your style, how do you write their performance review?

Here is the section where everything preceding comes together. In well-structured and tempered performance reviews, all four tonal categories should be used to draft your evaluation, especially when you must review a poor performer. This includes the involvement of using YOU, WHAT and WANT in your review. Knowing this, I present what I have seen as one of the best templates to address any type of performer. May it help you draft your next performance review with credibility, respectability and professionalism.

HOW TO NAVIGATE TONAL CATEGORIES FOR PERFORMANCE REVIEWS

For giving praise, use Active Voice and a mixture of formal and informal language.

When addressing areas of development, use formal and indirect language.

To review incidents, stick to Passive Voice as much as possible.

For any call to action, use formal and direct language while minimizing the use of YOU, WHAT, and WANT.

If at all possible, end on a positive note.

Some managers, particularly senior managers, might scoff at the above formula in light of colleagues who are simply poor performers. If you are one of those managers, I really do sympathize with you. One of the worst collegial actions is having to overcompensate your time and energy to mend poor performance. In saying that, if you want the performance from your colleague to improve, will dehumanizing your teammate be the best motivator? So, I ask you here: what is your goal with the draft of your performance review of a colleague who is performing poorly? If your immediate goal is to dehumanize, soul-crush, and verbally shank your teammate, do you really believe that a better performance will sprout from your actions?

As someone who was raised by Jamaicans in a Caribbean household, tough love **is no stranger to** my upbringing. I was literally born into an environment in which tough love was meant as a protective shield: a course designed to prepare young black daughters to face racists, bigots, and bullying men. Furthermore, I also went to art school nearly all of my life in which a founding principle of art school is the subjugation to critiques. So, when I say that negative or critical evaluation is not about issuing damning insults, I say this from many, many, many years of both personal and professional experience.

Being tough is not about how well you insult your opponent, peer, or even enemy (dare I say). Being tough is about how well you can take life's correctional beatings in order to raise the vulnerable up alongside you as you rise and rise again.

Mouthy performance evaluators, who use all forms of rude language to rip apart their colleagues, disgust me to my core. They are cowards—all of them. These bullying harassers wouldn't last 2 days in a Caribbean household—nevertheless 2 hours! It just makes me laugh. Their behaviors are indicative of a past rot in uncontrolled and unaddressed insecurities. Perhaps the following expression exposes the reason as to why: "Hurt people hurt people." In this dictation, the first "hurt" is an adjective. The second "hurt" is a verb. Those who have not found healing from past hurts often tend to find ways to hurt others.

So, if you are tempted to write an unprofessional and aggressive evaluation: get over yourself and man up. Get over yourself and woman up. Instead, negatively evaluate poor performers honorably. That is the real challenge.

If you must conduct a performance evaluation in English, remember the lessons, advice, and strategies from above. If you want to provoke your colleague or subordinate into better performance, I am over 95% sure verbal decimation will achieve the very opposite response. We have all seen colleagues tank from poorly crafted performance reviews with language that would be a light slap on the wrist if issued to another. In saying that, neither do I support sugarcoating poor performance either. So if your goal is to cultivate better performance, then master the tonal categories in English and draft a critically constructive review of what was lacking in the performance.

Simply put, direct communication depends on what outcome you'd like or expect. If you want to motivate your staff, peers, or even your superiors, then perhaps insulting their integrity is counterintuitive, even if you are aware that they deliberately underperform due to something like tenure. You are in control of your language. Why work in team-oriented environments if your goal is to encourage demotivation?

AFTERWARD

IT'S *not* TOO LATE FOR ME

It was both a pleasure and a struggle to write this book. This book has not been written merely to teach you how to be a better professional communicator; it has been written to provide strategic advice on using and managing professional communication in toxic work environments, especially for people of color and members of protected classes. With it, I hope that you will be able to buy time to find out what you do well in order to launch a business of your own or reach career benchmarks from your dreams.

Since 2017, I have been traveling around the world in order to study key languages in the region of my target language. I aim to learn Russian, French, German, and Spanish. These languages come across my dossier the most as I continue to ascend the career ladder in International Affairs so that I may work more effectively as a Humanitarian Advisor, ideally in West Africa. While studying, I have taken on private clients at corporations and organizations to teach professional communication skills as a consultant on Strategic Communications. While coaching, my clients are usually surprised to learn about my language learning goals and the journey that I have **set up** to achieve my **career objective**. They are not alone. Whether someone is moved by genuine interest or, sadly, by prejudice, skepticism, and nationalism, the language that seems to shock inquirers the most is Russian.

"What? Russian? What do you mean by learning Russian? Are you sure that you need this?"

Nowadays, I share this story for an answer:

At the beginning of 2019, the International Committee of the Red Cross (ICRC) was searching for a Public Relations Officer in Dakar, Senegal. As usual, I skipped the job description and **headed straight down** to the job requirements. For this job advertisement, French was listed as the first language requirement, followed by, "[a] very good working knowledge of English." Immediately after this, the job posting said, "German, Russian, and/or Spanish [would be] an asset." This job description was the first time that I had seen all five of my target languages required for one position. To me, the job posting was indicative of one megatrend: The world is globalizing.

In my field, despite being a native English speaker, I am **barred** from career-advancing opportunities because I lack fully developed foreign language skills. Ten to fifteen years ago, I would have thought it was impossible to acquire a new language. Now, thanks to social media, polyglots around the world have shared their language learning journeys and best practices used to acquire a new language.

Yes, students who began their foreign language journey early on in life have already prepared their minds for acquiring a new language. On the other hand, for adults who start their foreign language journey later on in life, it is crucial **to bear in mind** that many others have chosen to do so too—and have succeeded! I say this because there are many theories about how adults are unable to acquire foreign language skills after childhood.

I have seen these theories shattered **time and time again** by using simple learning methods based on discipline and repetition. You don't need to be a genius; you do need to be persistent, repetitive, and, most importantly, understand how you learn best! So, if you have chosen to start your foreign language learning journey in your adulthood, then you are not alone. It is possible to learn a foreign language to fluency after childhood.

And no, this skill is not predicated on talent; instead, foreign language skills are acquired based on how you learn best and repetition. For me, I am a kinesthetic learner and prefer using right-brained and creative mythologies to learn anything. I specialize in teaching clients who learn similarly; they are usually the ones who struggled to grasp concepts in schools that relied on blackboards and textbooks to transmit learning methodologies.

We poor fellows, whose anxieties run high if exposed only to visual or auditory material without guidance, miss much under traditional curricula. As such, I teach my clients by using physically engaging techniques that lean toward creative thinkers. Thus, the clients who benefit most from my teaching-style seem to be those who were not successful at learning a language during their schooling.

Traditional schooling favors left-brained thinkers and left-brained methodologies. For example, learning a foreign language during primary and secondary education in America used a rota-style process for vocabulary acquisition and a plug-in grammar-building system. After reviewing the list of rules for each grammar principle, students were expected to select and fill in the properly conjugated answer. The traditional approach is not effective for those who learn by using more physical interactions with newly acquired skills.

No amount of logical adaptation will ever penetrate a mind that wanders freely between abstract concepts and concrete thinking. In essence, artistic mindsets learn by using experiential tasks. Either learning style may feel pragmatic and methodological when the method is properly applied to the right learner.

If you have felt overwhelming difficulties in acquiring a language, perhaps you may adapt better to another learning methodology. So, clients adapt well to my teaching methods because I tailor every lesson to each client's immediate learning needs, whether it be visual, auditory, or kinesthetic in approach. My lessons use sensory experiences to enhance physical engagement with newly acquired knowledge. Instead of assigning homework, exercises are repeated multiple times in order to reinforce retention. That is (of course) unless the client wants homework. But who on earth really has time for homework when being an adult comes to call?

Relevant + Hands-on + Repetition = Lesson Learnt.

DEBUNKING PATRIOTISM AND HATE SPEECH

I fervently believe that it is foolish to think foreign language skills disgrace our nationalities or shame our identities. On the contrary, the ability to express yourself in another's native tongue solidifies who you are, what you believe and how you think.

Social media has expanded our reach into the lives of others across continents. The medium has become both an instrument for positive change and a fatally disastrous instigator for radicalizing hate. On the positive end, the medium has helped to dispel and confront our bigotries, prejudices, and worse impulses about our foreign neighbors abroad. Moved by the stories from across the globe, a distant glimpse into the lives of others shrinks our emotional differences and expands our intellectual capacities to empathize. By doing so, the world does not seem so very large.

And yet, social media has also achieved the exact opposite in results. Once again, global communities are combating a populist-backed movement to revamp a fashion trend of racism, bigotry, and hate speech in order to satiate histrionic outbursts that are rooted in generational discrimination. Normalized by public figures, hate speech explores a resurgence of institutionalized terrorism whilst simultaneously watering seeds of hereditary prejudices.

A deeper look into hate speech was commissioned by the United Nations in 2018 to E. Tendayi Achiume, Special Rapporteur on contemporary forms of racism, racial discrimination, xenophobia, and related intolerance. The Special Rapporteur concluded that the urgency to relook at how hate speech is encouraged—**from the top-down**—is vital to the safety and social health of our communities, particularly for those who are living under the protection of the establishment.

Hate speech imprisons, limits, controls, and destroys those to whom it targets. I don't see it as a protected right; I see it as an unregistered license to commit legalized terrorism. That is one of the least patriotic behaviors a society can defend.

PUTTING IT ALL TOGETHER

In spite of my message above, diplomatic speeches will not solve the underlying drivers behind hate. From the top-down, accusations of these behaviors are defended or dismissed. From the bottom up, an unrelenting fight against legalized bigotry is censored, diluted, and undermined.

Prejudices and discriminatory behaviors are taught in speech and by actions acquired at home along the family tree. Hereditary bigotry is the most dangerous and unrecognized generational curse of the 21st century. Diplomacy will not stop it. Suppression will not stop it. Denial will not stop it. White Guilt will not fix it.

Here is where, *Give Me Tea, Please* **fails with flying colors** in its delivery. Truly, tactful and cultured language has the power to calm, to reason, to amend disagreements, and to ease tension. But bigotry is only defeated by education.

So, when dealing with hate speech and spiteful colleagues or suffocating in toxic work environments, use *Give Me Tea, Please*, to form a protective and diplomatic shell around you. Practice the techniques so that you may stand blameless against those who would wield the power of bigotry against you. Don't be fooled or caught off guard; your professional adversaries will be doing the same thing against you.

Best of luck!

SPILL THE TEA!

If you enjoyed this book, I would like to gently ask for your reviews on Amazon, Goodreads, and Facebook, particularly in book recommendation groups. Your thoughtfulness helps support artists and creators like me in our budding stages of a creative profession. I deeply value and sincerely appreciate your ongoing support.

REFERENCES

THE ENCYCLOPEDIA OF PROFESSIONAL COMMUNICATION

Expand your colloquialisms, phrasal verbs, and new professional vocabulary as you reference the words in bold with this section. I encourage you to use dictionaries written in simple and basic form. Unless indicated with an asterisk, the following definitions were taken from my favorite online dictionaries.

CAMBRIDGE DICTIONARY
Excellent for non-native English speakers with very simplistic and easy to understand definitions.
Cambridge Dictionary. (2021). Cambridge University Press. https://dictionary.cambridge.org

MERRIAM-WEBSTER
An advanced-level dictionary that is well suited for academics.
Merriam-Webster. (2021). Merriam-Webster. https://www.merriam-webster.com

MACMILLAN
One of the best resources for definitions of phrases, idioms, and phrasal verbs.
Macmillan Dictionary. (2009–2021). Macmillan Education Limited. https://www.macmillandictionary.com

WORDS IN BOLD

a little goes a long way: used to say that a small amount will be enough

abuse of power: taking advantage of another by using undue influence (often political influence) or seniority*

across the board: embracing or affecting all classes or categories

addressee: the recipient*

articulate: expressing oneself readily, clearly, and effectively; to utter clear and understandable sounds

artistic licenses: the freedom to break traditional rules and principles or repurpose elements as the creator see fits

as soon as possible: abbreviated form is ASAP*

at a loss for words: unable to think of anything to say

at all costs: regardless of the cost or consequences

at the helm of: to be in charge of a mission, project or organization*

back and forth: consideration of a question in open and usually informal debate; a usually good-natured exchange (as of ideas or comments)

be that as it may: an idiomatic phrase used at the beginning of a statement to show an alternative point of view.

bear (one's) soul: to reveal one's most private thoughts and feelings

bequeath: to transmit, give or leave an object to another person

blunders: accidents and mistakes

brief / brevity: very short form of communication*

brush-bys: short quick 15-minutes stand-up meetings*

buzzwords: keywords to use in job application, particularly for resumes, motivational letters, cover letters*

career objective: the overall career goal(s)*

challenging colleague: a colleague with whom is difficult to work*

child's play: an extremely simple task or act

clout: strong influence

colloquialism: everyday, conversational speech

comparatively: to make a comparison between two or more elements*

conducted: the way someone organizes or does something

corporate ladder: the career track to rise in rank within an industry or field*

corrosive: very toxic and destructive*

counterbalance: to oppose (someone or something) with equal force*

courtesy: polite behavior, or a polite action or remark

crucial: extremely important or necessary

day-to-day: happening every day as part of your normal life

debasing: causing a lowering of someone or something in status, esteem, quality, or character

demote: to lower one's professional rank*

diary: a British term meaning schedule or calendar*

digest: to understand a concept, to swallow*

dominates: to have the most superior influence*

dossier: a collection of documents that contains information relating to a person or subject

earnings: wages, salary*

estimate: to make an educated guess*

face value: to accept the impression that someone gives of themselves, even though this may be completely false*

fail/pass with flying colors: if you do something with flying colors, you do it extremely well

fake it till you make it: purport yourself however you please to in order to get what you want*

fall short: to fail to reach an amount or standard that was expected or hoped for, causing disappointment

faux pas: mistakes*

fictitious: invented and not true or not existing

flat out: as quickly or with as much effort as possible

fluidly: easily movable*

for all intents and purposes: used for saying that although something is not exactly true or accurate, the situation is the same as if it were true or accurate

for the long haul: determined to continue with something until it is finished successfully

fruition: the state of having successfully completed an activity or plan

funnily enough: used for saying that you think something is surprising or unusual

game plan: a strategy for achieving an objective

garner: to collect something, usually after much work or with difficulty

get straight to the point: to stop talking about unimportant details and say what is most important

globalize: develop or be developed so as to make international influence or operation possible*

go-to: someone or something that is regularly or repeatedly chosen or employed for reliably good results

gossip: to say unverified information*

honey traps: to clandestinely trap someone in a romantic and seductive way*

in no uncertain terms: in a way that is clear and definite

in question: concerning the person or object being discussed*

in sheep's clothing: an untrustworthy person disguised as honorable*

in the belly of the beast: the most dangerous part of a situation*

in the lion's den: in the heart of danger*

inventive: very good at thinking of new and original ideas

join forces: to start to work together in order to achieve a shared goal

key: someone or something very important*

lean on: to depend on someone or something*

liable: likely*

like a blunt ax: an action performed without sensitivity*

lucrative: profitable*

midway through the game: the halfway point until an action is completed*

mind your ps and qs: be polite*

mind's eye: in your imagination or memory

missteps: mistakes*

neither...nor: a correlative conjunction in grammar used to show that no option is considerable*

no matter what: used to emphasize that something is always true, or that someone must do something

no offense given, none taken: a popular expression used to mean that a person is not upset by a potentially offensive comment*

no-brainer: not difficult to understand*

nod in the right direction: a non-verbal clue as to what choice or direction is right or best

not my cup of tea: a person, object or situation that is not likable*

on a equal footing: in conditions where everyone has an equal chance

on the other hand: to consider a second option*

on the whole: used for talking about the general situation

open the floor: an introductory statement to take questions and provide answers to an audience*

operational challenge: difficulties in completing a task*

overtly: used about feelings and opinions that are expressed in a very open way

peculiar: strange*

peer: your equality in social environment*

per se: considered by itself: used for emphasizing that you are not considering something in relation to anything else

peremptory: (especially of a person's manner or actions) expecting to be obeyed immediately and without any questions

perfunctory: robotic in behavior or function*

period: used for emphasis to show that there is no more to be said about something

persuasive: the ability to influence a person's thoughts and behaviors*

pervaded: to spread throughout all parts*

post: another word for job or position*

postponed: to delay*

precarious: characterized by a lack of security or stability that threatens with danger

private practice: one's ownership of a business*

projected: planned for the future or calculated based on information already known

propose: to suggest a new option or idea*

protected classes: a group of people protected under a specific law*

putting two and two together: understanding how two different aspects logically work together*

Q&A: a session or segment the take questions and provide answers*

raise any eyebrows: to cause surprise or shock

reading an environment: to use your senses to understand the social dynamics of a room*

reframe:: to retell (a story) in a new way*

respectively: used for saying that something happens separately to each of the people or things mentioned in the order in which they were mentioned

retain: to keep or continue to have something

retains: to keep something*

rule of thumb: a method of procedure based on experience and common sense; a general principle regarded as roughly correct but not intended to be scientifically accurate

salutation: a greeting used at the beginning of a communique or oral presentation*

seeking out: to find*

seldom: rarely*

set up: to arrange*

should do the trick: to achieve what you want*

sow the seeds: to make a process begin to develop*

spill the tea: to share good or bad information that is often gossip, confidential or private.

stagnate: to stay the same and not grow or develop

stark difference (stark contrast): a very noticeable and clear difference between two or more things*

steering clear of: to not be involved*

stick to the facts: a direct expression that means to only be factual*

take note: to document*

take the bait: to be led into a trap*

taking the initiative: to do something (an action) before being asked to do so*

target audience: (one's) main audience*

the devil is in the details: the details of a seemingly simple matter are its most problematic aspect*

the end of the line: the end of a situation or condition

the tangled web: an extremely complicated and difficult situation to understand*

throw you under the bus: cause someone else to suffer in order to save oneself or gain personal advantage*

time and time again: to do something repetitively*

time to time: occasionally*

to be barred: to prevent access to something*

to be crossed: to be angry

to be no stranger to (something): to be familiar with someone or something*

to bear in mind: to remember*

to boil down: to go to the main points*

to break away from: to leave*

to err on the side of caution: be careful*

to feed off: to use something in order to continue to exist or become stronger

to have (one's) day in court: to get the opportunity to defend yourself from criticism

to have agency: the capacity, condition, or state of acting or of exerting power; a person or thing through which power is exerted or an end is achieved

to head straight down: to go directly to a location without detours*

to nail down: to secure*

top-down: controlled by the people with the highest status in an organization

to plant the seed: to suggest gently, to influence*

to pop up: to suddenly appear or occur*

to put (someone) on the spot: to cause embarrassment or difficulty by forcing someone at the moment to answer a difficult question or make an important decision

to put in a nutshell: to summarize*

to put into practice: the try to do something in earnest*

to ramble: to talk without purpose*

to take leave: a formal way to say "depart"*

to toe the line: to follow the rules carefully*

to twist/wind (someone): to anger someone*

to work in (someone's) favor: to be profitable for someone*

try it out: informal and familiar way of saying "to try"

turnaround: the amount of time it takes to complete a task and return it to the requestor*

under the gun: to be under immense pressure*

uninhibited: to move freely*

valediction: a formal way to say goodbye in a speech or written correspondence*

wags a finger: to chastise and correct especially in a condescending manner*

when the going gets tough: and expression meaning when times are difficult*

whether or not: used when someone does not know which of two possibilities is true

whichever/whatever floats your boat: whatever you like*

you catch more flies with honey than vinegar: be kind to get what you want*

you have your head on your shoulders: to be intelligent and able to make good decisions

you, what, want: the most dangerous words in professional vocabulary*

SALUTATIONS AND VALEDICTIONS

Contacting new colleagues or acquaintances is an opportunity to present your best self. Keep your opening lines positive. In situations where you simply don't know what to say, try: "I hope this email/message/greeting finds you well." Be creative. Try scripting your own general openers.

FORMAL	SALUTATIONS	INFORMAL
Dear Greetings Welcome		Hey, Hi, Yo, etc. *(Very informal and should only be used with friends)*
To whom it may concern *(a bit outdated)*		Hello
Good morning Good evening Good afternoon		Morning all Evening all Afternoon all

FORMAL	SALUTATIONS	INFORMAL
Sir/Madame		
Mr. Last name (Used for men)	First name only	
Ms. Last name (Used for all women regardless of marital status. More commonly used in contemporary times due to politically correct culture)		
Mrs. Last name (Used for married women only)		
Miss Last name (Used for unmarried, young women. This title is a tad bit outdated but still commonly appears with an older crowd.)		

Contacting new colleagues or acquaintances is an opportunity to present your best self. Keep your opening lines positive. In situations where you simply don't know what to say, try: "I hope this email/message/greeting finds you well." Be creative. Try scripting your own general openers.

FORMAL	VALEDICTIONS	INFORMAL	
Thank you Sincerely (quite standard) Cordially (very professional)	Thanks Many thanks		
Regards (rigidly formal) Kind regards Kindest regards	Best		
Humbly yours	Always All my love With love	*Very personal and should be used only with friends.*	

www.ingramcontent.com/pod-product-compliance
Lightning Source LLC
Chambersburg PA
CBHW060324130626
46553CB00003B/911